NAVIGATING PERSONAL INJURY LAW

# FROM INJURY TO COMPENSATION AND BEYOND

*The Complete Guide to Personal Injury Claims in New [illegible] rnia*

NGOZI E. BOLIN, ESQ.

# Legal Disclaimer

**IMPORTANT: PLEASE READ CAREFULLY**

The information contained in this book is provided for general informational and educational purposes only. Nothing in this publication constitutes legal advice, nor is it intended to do so. The content presented herein should not be used as a substitute for competent legal counsel from a licensed attorney in your jurisdiction.

**NO ATTORNEY-CLIENT RELATIONSHIP**

Reading this book, accessing its content, or implementing any suggestions contained within does not create an attorney-client relationship between the reader and the author, publisher, or any other party associated with this publication. No attorney-client privilege is established through the use of this material.

**NOT LEGAL ADVICE**

The information provided in this book is not legal advice and should not be construed as such. Laws vary significantly by jurisdiction and are subject to change. The application of legal principles depends heavily on the specific facts and circumstances of each individual case.

**CONSULT QUALIFIED COUNSEL**

Readers should consult with a qualified attorney licensed to practice in their jurisdiction before taking any action based on information contained in this book. Only a licensed attorney who is familiar with the laws of your jurisdiction and the specific facts of your situation can provide appropriate legal advice.

**NO WARRANTIES**

The author and publisher make no representations or warranties regarding the accuracy, completeness, or currency of the information contained in this book. Legal standards and requirements may change, and readers are responsible for ensuring they obtain current legal guidance.

**LIMITATION OF LIABILITY**

To the fullest extent permitted by law, the author, publisher, and all associated parties disclaim any liability for damages of any kind arising from the use of or reliance upon the information contained in this book.

By reading this book, you acknowledge that you have read and understood this disclaimer and agree to its terms.

# Contents

# Introduction: Your Roadmap to Recovery and Justice

## *A Simple Guide to Getting Justice After an Injury*

---

### What This Book Will Do for You

If you're reading this book, chances are you or someone you care about has been injured due to someone else's negligence. You may be feeling overwhelmed, confused, and uncertain about your rights. You're not alone – and you've come to the right place.

*From Injury to Compensation - And Beyond* is your comprehensive guide through the complex world of personal injury law, specifically tailored for those navigating claims in New York and California. This isn't just another legal textbook filled with incomprehensible jargon. It's a practical, step-by-step roadmap designed to empower you with the knowledge you need to protect your rights and secure fair compensation.

### What You Can Expect to Learn

This guide will take you through every stage of the personal injury process, from the critical first moments after an accident to the final resolution of your claim. You'll discover:

**Immediate Action Steps:** What to do in the first 24-48 hours after an injury to protect both your health and your legal rights. These early decisions can make or break your case.

**Legal Fundamentals:** Clear explanations of key concepts like negligence, comparative fault, and statutory deadlines - without the legal jargon that makes most people's eyes glaze over.

**State-Specific Guidance:** Detailed information about how New York's no-fault insurance system differs from California's at-fault approach, and what these differences mean for your claim.

**Insurance Navigation:** How to deal with insurance adjusters, avoid common traps, and recognize tactics designed to minimize your compensation.

**Documentation Strategies:** What evidence to preserve, how to build a compelling case file, and why your personal injury journal could be worth thousands of dollars.

**Settlement vs. Trial:** When to accept an offer, when to hold firm, and how to recognize if your case should go to court.

**Financial Protection:** How to calculate your true damages, handle medical liens, understand tax implications, and plan for your financial future.

## Why This Book Is Different

Unlike generic personal injury guides, this book focuses specifically on the laws, procedures, and practical realities in New York and California - two states with vastly different approaches to personal injury claims. You'll get targeted advice that applies directly to your situation, not generic information that may or may not be relevant.

More importantly, this guide is written from the perspective of someone who has been in the trenches for over three decades. The author doesn't just know the law - she knows how it works in practice, what insurance companies really think about, and what strategies actually succeed in real-world negotiations and courtrooms.

## A Word About Your Author

This guide comes from Ngozi E. Bolin, Esq., a seasoned trial attorney with over 30 years of litigation experience across multiple jurisdictions. Admitted to practice in New York (1991) and California (2013), Ms. Bolin brings a unique international perspective, having also been admitted as a Barrister & Solicitor of the Supreme Court of Nigeria and educated under both the British Commonwealth system and at Harvard Extension School.

Throughout her distinguished career, Ms. Bolin has successfully negotiated countless settlements and tried cases involving personal injury, medical malpractice, employment law, and complex litigation. Her work on notable cases has been recognized in published court decisions, and her practical approach emphasizes achieving favorable outcomes through strategic thinking rather than prolonged battles.

What sets Ms. Bolin apart is her philosophy that knowledge should be accessible and affordable. She believes that understanding your rights shouldn't require a law degree, and that a great settlement often surpasses a lengthy court battle. This book embodies that philosophy - giving you the tools to make informed decisions about your case.

## How to Use This Guide

This book is organized to serve both as a step-by-step manual and a reference resource. If you're dealing with a fresh injury, start with the emergency checklist and work through the early chapters sequentially. If you're already deep in the claims process, jump to the sections most relevant to your current situation.

Each chapter builds on the previous ones, but they're also designed to stand alone when you need quick answers to specific questions. Key terms are defined in context and collected in a comprehensive glossary. State-specific information is clearly marked so you can focus on what applies to your jurisdiction.

## Important Disclaimers

Before we dive in, remember that this book provides general information and educational guidance - it is not legal advice specific to your situation. Laws change, cases are fact-specific, and every claim is unique. While this guide will make you a more informed consumer of legal services, it cannot replace the personalized advice of a qualified attorney familiar with your case.

Think of this book as your translator and advocate in understanding a complex system. It will help you ask better questions, recognize red flags, and make more informed decisions - but it cannot substitute for professional legal counsel when your case demands it.

## Your Journey Starts Here

Whether you're dealing with a car accident, slip and fall, medical malpractice, or any other type of personal injury, you have rights - and this book will help you understand and protect them. The legal system can be intimidating, but it doesn't have to be incomprehensible.

Your path from injury to compensation may not be easy, but it doesn't have to be traveled alone or in the dark. Let this guide be your companion as you navigate toward the justice and recovery you deserve.

The journey begins now. Let's get started.

# Quick Reference Emergency Guide

## *What to Do Right After an Accident*

---

IMMEDIATE ACTIONS (First 24-48 Hours)

**Your health and legal rights are at stake. Act quickly but carefully.**

### Medical Care First

- **Seek medical attention immediately**, even if you feel "fine" - adrenaline can mask serious injuries
- Some injuries (like concussions, soft tissue damage, internal bleeding) don't show symptoms right away
- Having immediate medical records strengthens your case and protects your health

### Document Everything

- **Take photos** of your injuries, the accident scene, any hazards, property damage, and vehicle positions
- Get **witness information**: full names, phone numbers, and email addresses

- Write down exactly what happened while it's fresh in your memory
- Save any damaged clothing, equipment, or personal items

### Official Reports Matter

- **File a police report** for any vehicle accident, regardless of severity
- **Report to management** for slip-and-falls, workplace accidents, or injuries on someone else's property
- Get a copy of any incident reports filed

### Protect Your Legal Position

- **Never give recorded statements** to insurance companies without speaking to a lawyer first
- **Don't apologize or admit fault** - even saying "I'm sorry" can be used against you later
- Insurance adjusters are trained to get you to say things that hurt your case

### Start Your Documentation

- **Begin a daily pain journal** - record pain levels (1-10 scale), symptoms, limitations, and how the injury affects your daily life
- This becomes crucial evidence of your suffering and recovery process

## CRITICAL DEADLINES YOU CANNOT MISS

**Missing these deadlines can destroy your case entirely, regardless of how strong it is.**

### New York Deadlines

- **10 days**: File DMV accident report if injury or property damage exceeds $1,000
- **30 days**: File no-fault (Personal Injury Protection) claim with your

auto insurer

- **45 days**: Medical providers must submit no-fault bills after treatment
- **90 days**: File notice of claim for injuries involving any government entity (city, state, federal)
- **2 years**: Wrongful death cases must be filed
- **2.5 years**: Medical malpractice cases must be filed
- **3 years**: Most other personal injury cases must be filed

### California Deadlines

- **10 days**: File DMV accident report if injury or property damage exceeds $1,000
- **6 months**: File government claim for injuries involving public entities
- **2 years**: Most personal injury cases must be filed

*These deadlines are absolute - courts will dismiss your case if you're even one day late.*

## INSURANCE: WHAT YOU MUST DO

### Immediate Notification

- **Call your insurance company within 24 hours** - failing to report promptly can void your coverage
- For auto accidents, exchange insurance information with all other drivers involved
- Get the **claim number and adjuster's direct contact** information

### Protect Yourself

- Provide basic facts but avoid detailed recorded statements without legal advice
- Insurance companies often try to settle quickly for far less than your case is worth

- Remember: The other party's insurance company is not on your side - their job is to pay you as little as possible

# EVIDENCE PRESERVATION

**Evidence disappears quickly - act now to preserve your case.**

## Physical Evidence

- **Don't throw away or clean** damaged clothing, equipment, or products that caused your injury
- Take photos of items before and after any necessary cleaning or repairs
- If a defective product caused your injury, stop using it and preserve it exactly as it was

## Medical Documentation

- **Keep every medical record, bill, and receipt** related to your injury
- Document all medical appointments, treatments, medications, and therapy sessions
- Track all injury-related expenses (transportation to medical appointments, medical equipment, etc.)

## Ongoing Documentation

- **Photograph visible injuries** regularly to show progression and healing
- **Record all missed work** and activities you can no longer participate in
- Keep a detailed calendar of how your injury affects your daily life

# PROTECT YOUR CLAIM FROM SABOTAGE

## Social Media Dangers

- **Limit or avoid posting** about your accident, activities, or recovery
- Insurance companies regularly monitor social media to find posts that contradict your injury claims
- Even innocent posts can be taken out of context and used against you

### Don't Fall for Common Traps

- **Never sign releases or settlement documents** without having an attorney review them first
- Quick settlement offers are usually far below what your case is actually worth
- Once you sign a release, you can never ask for more money, even if your injuries worsen

### Stay Organized

- Create a dedicated folder (physical and digital) for all accident-related documents
- **Follow all medical advice religiously** - insurance companies will argue that you're not really injured if you miss appointments or don't follow treatment plans

## WHEN TO CALL AN ATTORNEY IMMEDIATELY

**Don't wait - early legal intervention can make the difference between a fair settlement and getting nothing.**

### Serious Cases Requiring Immediate Legal Help

- **Any hospitalization or emergency room treatment**
- **Disputed fault** - when the other party or their insurance claims you caused the accident
- **Government entity involvement** (city buses, postal vehicles, government property)

- **Medical malpractice** - complex cases requiring expert witnesses
- **Defective products** causing injury
- **Multiple parties involved** in the accident

### Red Flags That You Need Legal Help

- Insurance company **pressuring you for a quick settlement**
- **Claim denied** or unreasonably delayed
- **Serious injuries** that will require ongoing treatment
- **Lost wages** exceeding a few days
- The other party's insurance company wants you to give a **recorded statement**

## FREE LEGAL RESOURCES

### No-Risk Consultations

- **Most personal injury attorneys offer completely free initial consultations**
- **No obligation** - you can get legal advice and decide later whether to hire them
- Many attorneys work on **contingency fee basis** - you pay nothing unless you win your case

### Why Early Legal Advice Matters

- **Even if you ultimately handle your own claim**, early legal guidance can prevent costly mistakes
- Attorneys know insurance company tactics and can level the playing field
- **Free consultation** can help you understand what your case is really worth

## KEY TAKEAWAYS

**Remember These Critical Points:**

1. **Act fast** - evidence disappears and deadlines are absolute
2. **Document everything** - photos, witnesses, medical care, pain levels
3. **Never admit fault** or give recorded statements without legal advice
4. **Don't trust quick settlement offers** - they're usually far too low
5. **Follow medical advice completely** - gaps in treatment hurt your case
6. **Consider legal help early** - free consultations can save you thousands

## IMPORTANT DISCLAIMER

This guide provides general information for emergency reference only. Personal injury law varies significantly by state and situation. **Always consult with a qualified personal injury attorney** in your jurisdiction for advice specific to your case. Time-sensitive deadlines and complex legal requirements make professional guidance essential for protecting your rights and maximizing your recovery.

**Remember: Insurance companies have teams of lawyers working to minimize what they pay you. Shouldn't you have someone fighting for your interests too?**

## CRITICAL DEADLINES: CALIFORNIA

- **10 days**: Report accident to DMV (if injury/property damage exceeds $1,000)
- **6 months**: File **Government Claim** (if injured by public agency or employee)
- **2 years**: File most **Personal Injury** claims

## INSURANCE NOTIFICATION

- Notify your insurer **as soon as possible** (preferably within 24 hours)

- After auto accidents: Exchange **insurance and contact info** with other drivers
- Request **claim number** and contact info for the assigned adjuster
- Keep detailed records of **all communications** with insurers

## EVIDENCE PRESERVATION

- Save all **damaged personal items** (clothing, gear, vehicles, products)
- Keep **medical records, bills, and receipts** organized and updated
- Take **progress photos** of injuries as they heal or worsen
- Document **out-of-pocket expenses**: Medications, transportation, caregiving, etc.
- Record **missed work**, lost income, and activity limitations

## PROTECT YOUR CLAIM

- Limit or avoid **social media** posts about the accident or your recovery
- Do **not sign any release or settlement** without legal review
- Create a **dedicated folder** (physical or digital) for all case-related documents
- Follow all **medical advice** and **attend appointments** consistently
- **Consult an attorney** before speaking with the other party's insurance company

## WHEN TO CALL AN ATTORNEY IMMEDIATELY

- Injuries requiring **hospitalization or surgery**
- **Disputed liability** or unclear fault
- Accidents involving **government agencies or vehicles**
- Cases involving **medical malpractice**

- **Product-related injuries** (e.g., faulty equipment, contaminated goods)
- When the insurance company is **pressuring for a quick settlement**
- **Complex accidents** involving multiple parties or unclear timelines

## FREE CONSULTATION RESOURCES

- Most personal injury attorneys offer **free initial consultations**
- Many work on a **contingency basis** (you don't pay unless you win)
- Even if you choose to handle your claim, **early legal advice** can prevent costly mistakes

**This guide is intended for emergency reference only. Please refer to the full chapters or consult an attorney for comprehensive legal guidance.**

# 1

# Understanding Personal Injury Law

*Why It Matters and Why It Helps You*

## What Is Personal Injury Law and Why Should You Care?

Personal injury law, also called tort law, is your legal safety net when someone else's actions cause you harm. Think of it as the rulebook that helps you get back on your feet after an accident that wasn't your fault. Whether you've been in a car crash, slipped at a grocery store, or been hurt by a defective product, personal injury law gives you the right to seek compensation for your injuries and losses.

**The Bottom Line:** If someone else's carelessness, recklessness, or intentional actions hurt you, you may be entitled to money to cover your medical bills, lost wages, pain and suffering, and other damages.

## How Personal Injury Cases Work: Civil vs. Criminal

Many people get confused about the difference between civil and criminal cases, especially when the same incident leads to both. Here's what you need to know:

### Criminal Cases

- **Who's involved:** The government prosecutes the wrongdoer
- **Purpose:** To punish the person who broke the law
- **Possible outcomes:** Jail time, fines, probation
- **Standard of proof:** "Beyond a reasonable doubt" (very high standard)
- **You don't control the case:** The prosecutor decides whether to file charges

### Civil Personal Injury Cases

- **Who's involved:** You (the injured person) sue the person who hurt you
- **Purpose:** To get you money to compensate for your losses
- **Possible outcomes:** Money damages, no jail time
- **Standard of proof:** "Preponderance of the evidence" (more likely than not - easier to prove)
- **You control the case:** You decide whether to file a lawsuit

**Real-World Example:** If a drunk driver hits you, they might face criminal charges for DUI (decided by the prosecutor) AND you can sue them separately for your medical bills and other damages (decided by you and your lawyer).

## The Four Building Blocks of a Personal Injury Case

To win a personal injury case, you typically need to prove four things. Think of them as the four legs of a chair - you need all four for your case to stand strong:

### 1. Duty of Care

The person who hurt you had a responsibility to act reasonably. Examples:

- **Drivers** must follow traffic laws and drive safely
- **Store owners** must keep their premises reasonably safe for customers
- **Doctors** must provide care that meets medical standards
- **Product manufacturers** must make reasonably safe products

## 2. Breach of Duty

The person failed to meet their responsibility. Examples:

- A driver texting while driving
- A store owner who doesn't clean up a spill
- A doctor who misdiagnoses an obvious condition
- A company that sells a product with known defects

## 3. Causation

The person's failure directly caused your injury. This has two parts:

- **Factual causation:** But for their actions, you wouldn't have been hurt
- **Legal causation:** Your injury was a foreseeable result of their actions

## 4. Damages

You suffered actual harm that can be measured in money. This includes:

- Medical expenses (past and future)
- Lost wages and earning capacity
- Pain and suffering
- Property damage
- Loss of enjoyment of life

# Types of Personal Injury Cases: What's Covered

Personal injury law covers many different situations. Here are the most common types:

## Motor Vehicle Accidents

**What it covers:** Car crashes, motorcycle accidents, truck accidents, pedestrian accidents, bicycle accidents

**Key points for consumers:**

- Most states require auto insurance for this reason
- Fault is usually determined by traffic laws and evidence from the scene
- Even minor accidents can result in significant medical bills
- Don't admit fault at the scene - let the insurance companies and lawyers figure it out

**What you should do:**

1. Seek medical attention immediately
2. Document everything (photos, witness contact info)
3. Report to your insurance company
4. Keep records of all expenses
5. Consider consulting a lawyer if injuries are serious

## Slip and Fall (Premises Liability)

**What it covers:** Injuries on someone else's property due to dangerous conditions

**Common scenarios:**

- Wet floors without warning signs
- Broken stairs or railings
- Poor lighting in parking lots

- Ice and snow not properly cleared
- Falling merchandise in stores

**Key points for consumers:**

- Property owners aren't automatically liable for every accident
- You must prove they knew or should have known about the dangerous condition
- Take photos of the hazard and your injuries immediately
- Report the incident to the property owner/manager

## Product Liability

**What it covers:** Injuries caused by defective or dangerous products

**Three types of defects:**

1. **Design defects:** The product is inherently dangerous as designed
2. **Manufacturing defects:** Something went wrong during production
3. **Warning defects:** Inadequate instructions or warnings about risks

**Examples:**

- Exploding electronics
- Contaminated food
- Defective car parts
- Dangerous toys
- Faulty medical devices

**Key points for consumers:**

- You don't need to prove the manufacturer was careless
- Keep the defective product if possible
- Document your injuries with photos and medical records

## Medical Malpractice

**What it covers:** Injuries caused when healthcare providers deviate from standard care

**Common examples:**

- Misdiagnosis or delayed diagnosis
- Surgical errors
- Medication mistakes
- Birth injuries
- Failure to obtain informed consent

**Key points for consumers:**

- Not every bad medical outcome is malpractice
- You must prove the provider fell below the standard of care
- These cases require expert medical testimony
- There are strict time limits for filing claims
- Medical malpractice insurance often covers these claims

## Workplace Injuries Beyond Workers' Compensation

**What it covers:** Work-related injuries involving third parties or intentional acts

**When you might have a personal injury claim:**

- Defective equipment made by another company
- Car accident while working caused by another driver
- Assault by a non-employee
- Toxic exposure due to another company's negligence

**Key points for consumers:**

- Most workplace injuries are covered only by workers' compensation

- You can't sue your employer for ordinary workplace negligence
- Third-party claims can provide additional compensation

### Assault and Battery

**What it covers:** Intentional harmful or offensive contact

**Key differences from other personal injury cases:**

- These are intentional acts, not accidents
- The perpetrator may also face criminal charges
- You can sue even if there are no criminal charges filed
- Collecting money can be challenging if the attacker has no assets

### Wrongful Death

**What it covers:** When someone's death is caused by another's negligence or intentional act

**Who can file:**

- Surviving spouses
- Children
- Parents (in some cases)
- Other dependents (varies by state)

**Types of damages:**

- Funeral and burial expenses
- Lost financial support
- Loss of companionship
- Medical bills before death

## Understanding Damages: What Money Can You Get?

If you win your personal injury case, you may be entitled to different types of damages:

## Economic Damages (Easy to Calculate)

**Medical Expenses:**

- Emergency room visits
- Hospital stays
- Surgery costs
- Doctor visits
- Physical therapy
- Prescription medications
- Medical equipment (wheelchairs, crutches)
- Future medical care

**Lost Income:**

- Wages missed while recovering
- Reduced earning capacity if permanently disabled
- Lost benefits (health insurance, retirement contributions)
- Self-employment income losses

**Property Damage:**

- Vehicle repairs or replacement
- Damaged personal belongings
- Clothing destroyed in the accident

## Non-Economic Damages (Harder to Calculate)

**Pain and Suffering:**

- Physical pain from injuries

- Emotional distress
- Anxiety and depression
- Loss of enjoyment of life
- Scarring and disfigurement

**Relationship Damages:**

- Loss of companionship with spouse
- Inability to maintain family relationships
- Loss of consortium (intimate relationship with spouse)

### Punitive Damages (Rare)

- Only awarded in cases of extreme misconduct
- Designed to punish the wrongdoer and deter others
- Examples: drunk driving, intentional harm, corporate cover-ups

## State Law Differences: Why Location Matters

Personal injury law varies significantly from state to state. Here are key differences that affect your case:

### Fault Systems

**Pure Comparative Negligence (New York):**

- You can recover damages even if you're 99% at fault
- Your award is reduced by your percentage of fault
- Example: If you're 30% at fault in a $100,000 case, you get $70,000

**Pure Comparative Negligence (California):**

- Similar to New York but with some procedural differences
- Focus on economic vs. non-economic damages in certain cases

**Modified Comparative Negligence (Many states):**

- You can only recover if you're less than 50% or 51% at fault
- If you exceed the threshold, you get nothing

**Contributory Negligence (Few states):**

- If you're even 1% at fault, you get nothing
- Very harsh rule used in only a handful of jurisdictions

### Damage Caps

Some states limit how much you can recover for certain types of damages:

- **Medical malpractice caps:** Limits on pain and suffering awards
- **Punitive damage caps:** Limits on punishment awards
- **Wrongful death caps:** Limits on certain wrongful death damages

### Statutes of Limitations

Time limits for filing lawsuits vary by state and type of case:

- **Personal injury:** Typically 1-3 years from the date of injury
- **Medical malpractice:** Often 2-3 years, sometimes from discovery of injury
- **Product liability:** 2-4 years, may depend on when defect was discovered
- **Wrongful death:** Usually 2-3 years from date of death

## Red Flags: When You Definitely Need a Lawyer

While not every personal injury case requires an attorney, certain situations definitely warrant professional legal help:

### Serious Injuries

- Permanent disability or disfigurement
- Traumatic brain injuries

- Spinal cord injuries
- Injuries requiring multiple surgeries
- Injuries affecting your ability to work

### Complex Liability Issues

- Multiple parties potentially at fault
- Disputes about who caused the accident
- Commercial vehicle accidents
- Government entity involvement

### Insurance Company Problems

- Denial of obviously valid claims
- Unreasonably low settlement offers
- Delay tactics by insurance companies
- Bad faith insurance practices

### Significant Financial Stakes

- High medical bills
- Substantial lost income
- Expensive ongoing treatment needs
- Property damage exceeding policy limits

## Goals and Benefits of Personal Injury Law

Personal injury law serves several important purposes that benefit both individuals and society:

### Individual Benefits

**Full Compensation:** The law aims to make you "whole" again by compensating for all your losses, including:

- Every dollar of medical expenses
- All lost wages and future earning capacity
- Fair compensation for pain and suffering
- Replacement or repair of damaged property

**Access to Justice:** Personal injury law gives ordinary people the power to hold powerful entities (corporations, insurance companies, wealthy individuals) accountable for harm they cause.

**Peace of Mind:** Knowing you have legal recourse can provide psychological comfort during recovery.

### Societal Benefits

**Safety Incentives:** When companies and individuals know they'll be held financially responsible for the harm they cause, they're more likely to act safely.

**Cost Distribution:** Instead of leaving accident victims to bear the full cost of someone else's mistake, the law spreads these costs to those who caused the harm.

**Deterrence:** Public accountability for dangerous behavior helps prevent future accidents.

## Taking Action: Your Next Steps

If you've been injured due to someone else's actions, here's what you should do:

### Immediate Steps (First 24-48 Hours)

1. **Seek medical attention** - Even if you feel fine, some injuries don't show symptoms immediately
2. **Document everything** - Take photos of the scene, your injuries, and any property damage

3. **Get contact information** - Names and contact info for witnesses, other parties involved
4. **Report the incident** - To police (for accidents), property owners (for premises liability), or employers (for work injuries)
5. **Notify your insurance company** - Even if the accident wasn't your fault

### First Week

1. **Keep detailed records** - Medical appointments, expenses, time off work
2. **Don't give recorded statements** - Especially to the other party's insurance company
3. **Don't sign anything** - Except for medical releases from your own attorney
4. **Follow medical advice** - Missing appointments or treatments can hurt your case

### Ongoing

1. **Consider legal consultation** - Many personal injury lawyers offer free consultations
2. **Be patient** - Personal injury cases can take months or years to resolve
3. **Focus on recovery** - Your health is more important than your case

## Common Myths About Personal Injury Law

**Myth:** "Personal injury lawsuits are just about getting rich quick." **Reality:** Most personal injury awards barely cover the actual costs of medical care and lost wages. Very few cases result in "windfall" payments.

**Myth:** "You can sue for anything." **Reality:** You must have actual damages and prove someone else was at fault. Frivolous lawsuits are quickly dismissed.

**Myth:** "Insurance will cover everything." **Reality:** Insurance companies are businesses focused on profit, not paying claims. They often offer far less than claims are worth.

**Myth:** "Personal injury lawyers are just ambulance chasers." **Reality:** Reputable personal injury attorneys provide essential services helping injured people navigate complex legal and insurance systems.

**Myth:** "You have plenty of time to file a lawsuit." **Reality:** Statutes of limitations can be as short as one year. Waiting too long can destroy your case completely.

## Conclusion: Knowledge Is Power

Personal injury law exists to protect you when life takes an unexpected turn due to someone else's actions. Understanding your rights and the legal process empowers you to make informed decisions about your case and your future.

Remember, every situation is unique, and this guide provides general information that may not apply to your specific circumstances. When in doubt, consult with a qualified personal injury attorney who can evaluate your case and explain how the law applies to your situation.

The most important thing to remember is that you don't have to face the aftermath of an injury alone. The legal system provides tools and resources to help you recover and move forward with your life.

# 2

# Key Legal Concepts You Need to Know

*Basic Legal Terms Explained for Everyday People*

If you've been injured in an accident that wasn't your fault, understanding the basic legal principles can help you make informed decisions about your case. Personal injury law might seem complex, but the core concepts are actually quite straightforward once you break them down.

This guide will walk you through the fundamental legal building blocks that determine whether you have a valid claim and what compensation you might be entitled to receive.

## The Foundation: Four Elements Every Personal Injury Case Must Have

Think of these four elements as the pillars that support your entire case. If any one of them is missing, your claim may not succeed:

## 1. Duty of Care: Did They Owe You Safety?

This is about whether the person or entity that hurt you had a legal responsibility to keep you safe. In most situations, this duty exists naturally:

**Common Examples:**

- **Drivers** must follow traffic laws and drive safely around other vehicles and pedestrians
- **Store owners** must keep their floors clean and free of hazards that could cause customers to slip and fall
- **Doctors** must provide medical care that meets professional standards
- **Property owners** must maintain their premises so visitors aren't injured by dangerous conditions
- **Manufacturers** must design and produce safe products

**Real-World Scenario:** If you're walking through a grocery store and slip on a puddle of water that's been there for hours, the store owner had a duty to either clean it up or warn customers about the hazard.

## 2. Breach of Duty: Did They Fail in Their Responsibility?

This means showing that the responsible party didn't live up to their duty of care. They acted carelessly, recklessly, or failed to take reasonable precautions.

**What This Looks Like:**

- A driver texting while driving and running a red light
- A restaurant not cleaning up a spill after multiple customers complained
- A construction company not putting up proper warning signs around a work zone
- A landlord ignoring repeated requests to fix a broken staircase railing

**The "Reasonable Person" Test:** Courts often ask, "What would a reasonable person have done in this situation?" If the defendant's actions fall short of what a reasonable person would do, they've likely breached their duty.

## 3. Causation: Did Their Actions Actually Cause Your Injury?

This is often the most challenging element to prove because you must establish a clear connection between what they did wrong and your injury. There are two types of causation:

**Actual Cause (But-For Test):** Would your injury have happened if not for their actions? If you can honestly say "but for their careless driving, I wouldn't have been hurt," then actual cause is established.

**Proximate Cause (Foreseeability):** Was your injury a foreseeable result of their actions? If someone runs a red light, it's foreseeable that they might hit another car and injure the driver. However, if that accident somehow leads to a completely unrelated injury days later, proximate cause might be harder to prove.

**Example:** You're rear-ended at a traffic light because the other driver was speeding. Your whiplash injury has both actual cause (wouldn't have happened but for the speeding) and proximate cause (whiplash is a foreseeable result of rear-end collisions).

## 4. Damages: Did You Actually Suffer Harm?

You must have real, measurable losses that can be compensated with money. These fall into several categories:

**Economic Damages (Easy to Calculate):**

- Medical bills (hospital, doctor visits, physical therapy, medications)
- Lost wages from time off work
- Future medical expenses
- Lost earning capacity if you can't return to your previous job
- Property damage (car repairs, replacement of damaged items)

**Non-Economic Damages (Harder to Calculate):**

- Pain and suffering
- Emotional distress and mental anguish
- Loss of enjoyment of life activities

- Disfigurement or permanent disability
- Loss of consortium (impact on relationships)

**Punitive Damages (Rare but Significant):** These are awarded when the defendant's conduct was particularly reckless or intentional, designed to punish them and deter similar behavior.

## When Both Sides Share Blame: Understanding Comparative Negligence

Real life is complicated, and accidents often involve mistakes by multiple people. Fortunately, both New York and California have fair systems for handling shared fault.

### New York's Pure Comparative Negligence

New York has one of the most plaintiff-friendly systems in the country. Even if you were mostly at fault for your own accident, you can still recover some compensation.

**How It Works:**

- The jury determines what percentage of fault belongs to each party
- You receive compensation reduced by your percentage of fault
- Even if you're 99% at fault, you can still recover 1% of the damages

**Real Example:** You're crossing the street while looking at your phone and get hit by a speeding driver. The jury finds the total damages are $100,000 but determines you were 30% at fault for not paying attention. You would still receive $70,000.

### California's Comparative Fault System

California uses a similar approach, allowing injured people to recover damages proportionate to the other party's fault.

**Key Differences:**

- Multiple defendants can each be assigned different percentages of fault

- California courts may apply more nuanced interpretations in complex cases
- The system encourages settlements since both sides face some risk at trial

## Special Rules That Affect Your Case

### New York's No-Fault Insurance System

If you're injured in a car accident in New York, you'll first deal with the no-fault system before considering a lawsuit.

**How No-Fault Works:**

- Your own insurance pays for immediate expenses regardless of who caused the accident
- Coverage includes medical bills, lost wages (up to limits), and other out-of-pocket costs
- You cannot sue for pain and suffering unless your injuries are "serious"

**What Counts as a "Serious Injury" in New York:**

- Death
- Dismemberment
- Significant disfigurement
- Bone fractures
- Permanent limitation of body function
- Substantial disability lasting at least 90 days
- Pregnancy loss

**Why This Matters:** If your injuries don't meet the serious injury threshold, you may only recover economic damages through no-fault insurance. However, if you do meet the threshold, you can file a full lawsuit for all damages including pain and suffering.

### California's At-Fault System

California uses a traditional fault-based system where the responsible party pays for all damages.

**Minimum Insurance Requirements:**

- $15,000 for injury/death to one person
- $30,000 for injury/death to multiple people
- $5,000 for property damage

**Important Considerations:**

- These minimums are often inadequate for serious injuries
- You can pursue the at-fault driver's personal assets if insurance isn't enough
- Uninsured/underinsured motorist coverage protects you when others lack adequate insurance

## Beyond Negligence: Other Types of Personal Injury Claims

### Strict Liability Cases

Sometimes you don't need to prove negligence because the law automatically holds someone responsible.

**Common Strict Liability Situations:**

- **Defective products:** If a product is unreasonably dangerous, the manufacturer can be liable even if they weren't negligent
- **Dog bites:** In California, dog owners are automatically liable for bites, regardless of the dog's history
- **Abnormally dangerous activities:** Things like blasting with explosives or keeping wild animals

**Why This Matters:** Strict liability cases can be easier to win because you don't have to prove the defendant was careless - just that their product, animal, or activity caused your injury.

## Intentional Torts: When Someone Hurts You on Purpose

These cases involve deliberate actions meant to cause harm.

**Common Examples:**

- **Assault and battery:** Physical attacks or credible threats of violence
- **False imprisonment:** Unlawfully restraining someone against their will
- **Intentional infliction of emotional distress:** Extreme conduct that causes severe psychological harm
- **Defamation:** False statements that damage your reputation

**Key Difference:** You must prove intent, not just negligence. However, if successful, you might recover punitive damages in addition to compensatory damages.

## What You Need to Prove: The Burden of Evidence

In personal injury cases, you don't need to prove your case "beyond a reasonable doubt" like in criminal cases. Instead, you must meet the "preponderance of the evidence" standard.

**What This Means:**

- You must show it's more likely than not (greater than 50% chance) that your version of events is true
- Think of it as tipping the scales of justice slightly in your favor
- This is a much lower bar than criminal cases, making civil recovery more achievable

**Practical Impact:** Even if there's some uncertainty about exactly what happened, you can still win if your evidence is more convincing than the defendant's.

## Protecting Your Rights: Statutes of Limitations

Every state has deadlines for filing personal injury lawsuits. Missing these deadlines typically means losing your right to compensation forever.

**General Timeframes:**

- **New York:** Generally 3 years from the date of injury
- **California:** Generally 2 years from the date of injury
- **Medical malpractice:** Often has shorter deadlines and special rules
- **Government entities:** Usually much shorter deadlines (sometimes as little as 90 days)

**Why Acting Quickly Matters:**

- Evidence can disappear or deteriorate over time
- Witnesses' memories fade
- Medical records might be harder to obtain
- Insurance companies may be less cooperative as time passes

## Moving Forward: What This Means for Your Case

Understanding these legal concepts helps you:

**Evaluate Your Claim's Strength:**

- Do you have all four elements (duty, breach, causation, damages)?
- How strong is the evidence for each element?
- Could comparative negligence affect your recovery?

**Make Informed Decisions:**

- Whether to accept an insurance settlement offer
- Whether your case is worth pursuing in court
- What type of damages you might be entitled to receive

**Work More Effectively with Your Attorney:**

- Ask better questions about your case
- Understand their strategy and advice
- Participate more meaningfully in key decisions

**Set Realistic Expectations:**

- Understand what compensation might be available
- Appreciate the time and effort involved in pursuing a claim
- Recognize potential challenges or weaknesses in your case

## Key Takeaways

Personal injury law is designed to make injured people whole again by providing fair compensation for their losses. While the legal system can seem intimidating, the basic principles are grounded in common sense: if someone's carelessness or intentional actions hurt you, they should be responsible for the consequences.

Both New York and California have systems that allow you to recover compensation even if you bear some responsibility for your accident. The key is understanding your rights, gathering strong evidence, and acting within the required timeframes.

Remember that every case is unique, and this general information cannot replace personalized legal advice. If you've been injured, consulting with an experienced personal injury attorney can help you understand how these concepts apply to your specific situation and what options you have for recovery.

The next step in your journey will be understanding the specific deadlines and procedural requirements that govern when and how you must file your claim - critical information that can make or break your case regardless of how strong your underlying legal position might be.

# 3

# Understanding Your Legal Deadlines in New York and California

*Important Time Limits You Can't Afford to Miss*

## What You Need to Know Right Now

If you've been injured due to someone else's negligence, time is literally money. Every state has strict deadlines for filing personal injury lawsuits, and missing these deadlines can cost you everything - even if you have the strongest case imaginable.

**The Bottom Line:**

- **New York:** You typically have 3 years to file
- **California:** You typically have 2 years to file

- **But:** Many exceptions can shorten or extend these deadlines

This guide will help you understand exactly how much time you have and what factors might change your deadline.

# Understanding the Statute of Limitations

## What Is It?

The statute of limitations is like an expiration date on your legal rights. It's the maximum amount of time you have to file a lawsuit after an injury occurs. Once this deadline passes, courts will almost always refuse to hear your case, regardless of how badly you were hurt or how clearly the other party was at fault.

## Why Do These Deadlines Exist?

- **Evidence preservation:** Physical evidence deteriorates and disappears over time
- **Witness memory:** People's recollections fade and become less reliable
- **Fairness:** It protects defendants from having to defend against very old claims
- **Legal efficiency:** It encourages prompt resolution of disputes

## What Happens If You Miss the Deadline?

In nearly all cases, your lawsuit will be dismissed immediately. The court won't even look at the facts of your case. This is called being "time-barred," and it permanently ends your ability to seek compensation through the legal system

# Standard Time Limits by State

## New York Personal Injury Claims

**Standard Deadline: 3 Years from the Date of Injury**

**Real-World Example:** Sarah slips on ice outside a grocery store on February 10, 2024. She has until February 10, 2027, to file her lawsuit. If she files on February 11, 2027, her case will likely be dismissed.

**What Counts as the "Date of Injury":**

- Car accidents: The date of the crash
- Slip and falls: The date you fell
- Defective products: Usually the date you were first injured by the product
- Dog bites: The date of the attack

### California Personal Injury Claims

**Standard Deadline: 2 Years from the Date of Injury**

**Real-World Example:** Mike is injured in a bicycle accident on June 5, 2024. He must file his lawsuit by June 5, 2026. California's shorter deadline means less time to investigate, negotiate, and prepare your case.

**Important California Note:** The shorter 2-year deadline means you need to act more quickly than in many other states. Don't assume you have plenty of time to "figure things out later."

## Critical Exceptions That Can Change Your Deadline

### 1. The Discovery Rule: When You Don't Know You're Injured

Sometimes injuries or their causes aren't immediately apparent. Both New York and California recognize that it's unfair to start the clock ticking before you know you have a claim.

**When the Discovery Rule Applies:**

- Hidden medical malpractice (surgical instruments left inside patients)
- Toxic exposure cases (asbestos, chemical poisoning)
- Defective products with delayed effects

- Certain types of sexual abuse

**How It Works:** The statute of limitations begins when you discover (or reasonably should have discovered) both:

1. That you were injured, AND
2. That someone else's negligence likely caused your injury

**Real-World Example:** Jennifer has surgery in January 2020. In March 2024, she discovers the surgeon left a sponge inside her during the operation. Under the discovery rule, her statute of limitations likely begins in March 2024, not January 2020.

**Consumer Warning:** Don't assume the discovery rule applies to your case. It has strict requirements and doesn't apply to obvious injuries like car accidents or slip and falls.

## 2. Special Rules for Minors (Under 18)

Children can't file lawsuits on their own, so special rules protect their rights until they become adults.

**New York Rules for Minors:**

- The statute of limitations is "tolled" (paused) until the child turns 18
- Once they turn 18, they have 3 full years to file
- This means they have until age 21 to file their lawsuit

**California Rules for Minors:**

- The child has 2 years from their 18th birthday to file
- This means they have until age 20 to file their lawsuit

**Real-World Example:** Tommy, age 8, is injured in a school playground accident in California on September 1, 2024. He has until September 1, 2034 (age 20) to file a lawsuit. This gives his family plenty of time to understand the full extent of his injuries as he grows.

**Parent Alert:** Even though children have extended time limits, it's still wise to consult with an attorney early. Evidence can still disappear, and witnesses can become harder to locate over time.

## 3. Government Claims: Much Shorter Deadlines

Suing government entities (cities, counties, school districts, transit authorities) involves much stricter rules and shorter deadlines.

**New York Government Claims:**

1. **Notice of Claim:** Must be filed within 90 days of the incident
2. **Actual Lawsuit:** Must be filed within 1 year and 90 days of the incident

**California Government Claims:**

1. **Government Claim Form:** Must be filed within 6 months of the injury
2. **Court Lawsuit:** If your claim is denied, you have 6 months from the denial date to file in court

**Real-World Example:** Maria is hit by a city bus in San Francisco on January 15, 2024. She must file her government claim by July 15, 2024 (just 6 months later). If the city denies her claim on September 1, 2024, she has until March 1, 2025, to file her court lawsuit.

**Critical Consumer Alert:** Government claim deadlines are much shorter than regular personal injury deadlines. Many people lose their rights because they don't realize they're suing a government entity or don't understand the special procedures required.

**Who Counts as "Government":**

- City and county employees
- Public school districts
- Transit authorities (buses, subways)
- Public hospitals
- Police departments
- Fire departments
- Public universities

## 4. Medical Malpractice: Complex Rules

Medical malpractice cases have their own special deadlines because medical injuries are often discovered late or occur during ongoing treatment.

**New York Medical Malpractice:**

- **2 years and 6 months** from the date of malpractice, OR
- **2 years and 6 months** from the end of continuous treatment by the same provider

**California Medical Malpractice:** The earlier of:

- **3 years** from the date of injury, OR
- **1 year** from when you discovered (or should have discovered) the injury

**Additional California Requirement:** You must give the healthcare provider 90 days' written notice before filing your lawsuit.

**Real-World Examples:**

*New York:* Dr. Smith performs surgery on January 1, 2022, and continues treating the patient through December 1, 2022. The patient has until June 1, 2025 (2.5 years after treatment ended) to file.

*California:* A patient discovers in July 2024 that their 2021 surgery was botched. They have until July 2025 (1 year from discovery) to file, even though the surgery was over 3 years ago.

**Consumer Tip:** Medical malpractice cases are among the most complex in personal injury law. Always consult with a specialized medical malpractice attorney as soon as you suspect negligence.

## 5. Wrongful Death Claims

When someone dies from injuries caused by another's negligence, the family has a separate type of claim with its own deadline.

**Both New York and California:** 2 years from the date of death (not the date of injury)

**Real-World Example:** John is injured in a car accident on March 1, 2024, but dies from his injuries on June 1, 2024. His family has until June 1, 2026, to file a wrongful death lawsuit.

**Who Can File:**

- **New York:** Personal representative of the estate
- **California:** Surviving spouse, children, or other specified family members

## 6. Product Liability Claims

When you're injured by a defective product, standard personal injury deadlines usually apply, but the discovery rule may come into play.

**Standard Deadlines:**

- **New York:** 3 years
- **California:** 2 years

**When Discovery Rule Applies:**

- The defect wasn't obvious at the time of injury
- Health effects developed over time
- The connection between the product and injury wasn't immediately apparent

**Real-World Example:** A child's toy contains toxic paint that causes developmental issues over several years. The parents don't discover the connection until the child is diagnosed in 2024. The statute of limitations may begin in 2024 when they discovered the toy's role in their child's condition.

# Special Circumstances That Can Extend Deadlines

## Mental Incapacity

If you're declared legally incompetent due to mental illness or disability, the statute of limitations may be tolled until you regain capacity or a guardian is appointed.

## Defendant Leaves the State

In some cases, if the person who injured you leaves the state, the time they're gone might not count toward your statute of limitations.

### Fraudulent Concealment

If the defendant actively hides their wrongdoing, the statute of limitations might not begin until you discover their deception.

### Military Service

Active military duty can sometimes pause the statute of limitations under federal law.

## Red Flags: When Your Deadline Might Be Shorter

### Insurance Claims vs. Lawsuits

**Important:** Filing an insurance claim does NOT stop the statute of limitations clock. You must file an actual lawsuit in court to preserve your rights.

### No-Fault Insurance States

Even in no-fault insurance states, you may still need to file a lawsuit within the statute of limitations to preserve certain rights.

### Pre-Existing Relationships

Doctor-patient relationships, ongoing business relationships, or continuing care situations can complicate when the statute begins.

## Practical Steps to Protect Your Rights

### Immediate Actions (First 30 Days)

1. **Seek medical attention** - Document your injuries
2. **Gather evidence** - Photos, witness information, incident reports
3. **Keep detailed records** - Medical bills, lost wages, daily pain logs

4. **Report the incident** - To property owners, employers, or authorities
5. **Contact an attorney** - Many offer free consultations

### Within 90 Days

1. **File government notices** if applicable
2. **Preserve evidence** - Send preservation letters to defendants
3. **Continue medical treatment** - Follow all doctor recommendations
4. **Document everything** - Keep a detailed journal of your recovery

### Before Your Deadline

1. **File your lawsuit** - Don't wait until the last minute
2. **Complete medical treatment** - Or reach maximum medical improvement
3. **Calculate all damages** - Medical bills, lost wages, pain and suffering

## Common Consumer Mistakes to Avoid

### Mistake #1: Relying on Insurance Companies

**The Problem:** Insurance adjusters may tell you that you have "plenty of time" or that filing a lawsuit isn't necessary.**The Reality:** Insurance companies don't work for you. They may delay negotiations until your deadline passes.

### Mistake #2: Waiting for Medical Treatment to End

**The Problem:** Thinking you need to wait until you're "completely better" to file. **The Reality:** You can file a lawsuit while still receiving treatment. Waiting too long can cost you everything.

### Mistake #3: Assuming You Know Your Deadline

**The Problem:** Thinking all personal injury cases have the same deadline. **The Reality:** Medical malpractice, government claims, and other special cases have different rules.

### Mistake #4: Filing Insurance Claims Instead of Lawsuits

**The Problem:** Believing that filing an insurance claim preserves your legal rights. **The Reality:** Only filing an actual lawsuit in court stops the statute of limitations.

### Mistake #5: Waiting for the "Right Time"

**The Problem:** Hoping the other party will "do the right thing" without legal pressure. **The Reality:** Once your deadline passes, you have zero leverage.

## When to Consult an Attorney

### Consult Immediately If:

- You're injured by a government entity
- You suspect medical malpractice
- Your injuries are severe or permanent
- Multiple parties may be responsible
- The accident involved complex factors
- You're unsure about your deadline

### What to Bring to Your Attorney Consultation:

- All medical records and bills
- Photos of the accident scene and your injuries
- Contact information for witnesses
- Police reports or incident reports
- Insurance correspondence
- Documentation of lost wages
- A timeline of events

## Frequently Asked Questions

### Q: Can I file a lawsuit after settling with insurance?

**A:** Usually no. Most insurance settlements include a release that prevents you from filing a lawsuit. Read all settlement documents carefully before signing.

### Q: What if I discover new injuries after my deadline passes?

**A:** This is complicated and depends on many factors. In some cases, you may have a new claim for the newly discovered injuries, but don't count on it. Consult an attorney immediately.

### Q: Does filing a lawsuit mean I can't settle out of court?

**A:** No. Most lawsuits settle before trial. Filing a lawsuit preserves your rights while still allowing negotiation.

### Q: What if the person who injured me has no money or insurance?

**A:** You may still want to file suit to preserve your rights. You might discover other insurance coverage or responsible parties during the legal process.

### Q: Can I represent myself in a personal injury lawsuit?

**A:** Legally yes, but it's rarely advisable. Personal injury law is complex, and insurance companies have experienced lawyers working against you.

## Emergency Deadline Checklist

**If your deadline is approaching (within 30 days):**

☐ **Stop everything else** - This is your priority ☐ **Contact an attorney immediately** - Don't wait for Monday ☐ **Gather all your documents** - Medical records, photos, witness info ☐ **Don't sign anything** - Insurance releases, settlement offers, etc. ☐ **File your lawsuit** - Even if you're still negotiating ☐ **Preserve evidence** - Take photos, secure witness statements

**Remember:** It's better to file a lawsuit and settle later than to miss your deadline and lose everything.

## State-Specific Resources

### New York Resources

- New York State Bar Association: Lawyer referral services
- New York Courts: Self-help resources and forms
- Department of Financial Services: Insurance complaint process

### California Resources

- State Bar of California: Attorney referral services
- California Courts: Self-help resources
- Department of Insurance: Consumer assistance

## Final Thoughts: Time Is Your Most Valuable Asset

Your right to compensation after an injury is valuable, but it's also fragile. Unlike money or property, once you lose your legal rights due to missed deadlines, they're gone forever. No amount of evidence, no degree of fault by the other party, and no severity of injury can overcome a missed statute of limitations.

The key takeaways for consumers:

**Act Early:** Don't wait to see how you feel or hope the other party will do the right thing. Start the legal process early to preserve all your options.

**Get Professional Help:** Personal injury law is complex, and the stakes are high. A consultation with an experienced attorney can save you from costly mistakes.

**Document Everything:** From day one, treat your injury case like the important legal matter it is. Keep records, take photos, and preserve evidence.

**Don't Trust the Other Side:** Insurance companies and defendants have no obligation to remind you of your deadlines. They may even actively try to delay until your time runs out.

Remember: Filing a lawsuit doesn't mean you can't settle your case amicably. It simply preserves your right to seek full compensation if negotiations fail. In the world of personal injury law, it's much better to be safe than sorry.

*This guide provides general information about statute of limitations rules in New York and California. Laws can change, and every case is unique. Always consult with a qualified personal injury attorney in your state for advice about your specific situation.*

# 4

# Understanding Negligence and Fault

## *Who's At Fault and Why It Matters*

---

When you've been injured due to someone else's actions, understanding who's legally responsible - and why - can feel overwhelming. Whether you're dealing with a car accident, a slip and fall at a business, or an injury from a defective product, the heart of your potential case likely revolves around a legal concept called "negligence."

This guide will help you understand what negligence means in plain terms, how fault is determined, and what options you have for seeking compensation. We'll also explore situations where fault doesn't matter (strict liability) and cases involving intentional harm.

### What Is Negligence? Breaking It Down Simply

Think of negligence as carelessness that causes harm to others. In everyday terms, it means someone failed to act as carefully as a reasonable person would in the same situation, and that carelessness directly led to your injury.

Legally speaking, negligence has four essential parts that must all be present for a successful claim. Think of them as four links in a chain - if any link is missing, the chain breaks:

## The Four Elements of Negligence

1. **Duty of Care** Everyone has certain responsibilities to others in different situations. For example:

- Drivers must follow traffic laws and drive safely
- Store owners must keep their premises reasonably safe for customers
- Doctors must provide competent medical care
- Property owners must maintain their buildings in safe condition

The specific duty depends on the relationship between the people involved and the circumstances of the situation.

2. **Breach of Duty** This is where someone fails to meet their responsibility. They either did something they shouldn't have done, or failed to do something they should have done. The key question is: "Would a reasonable person have acted differently in this situation?"

Examples of breaching duty:

- A driver texting while driving
- A store leaving a spill on the floor for hours without cleaning it
- A construction company not following safety protocols
- A manufacturer skipping quality control tests

3. **Causation (The Connection)** You must prove that the other person's careless action directly caused your injury. This has two parts:

- **Actual cause**: The injury wouldn't have happened "but for" the defendant's actions
- **Proximate cause**: The injury was a foreseeable result of the defendant's actions

For instance, if someone runs a red light and hits your car, there's a clear connection between their action and your injuries. But if you were injured in a completely separate incident days later, that connection doesn't exist.

**4. Damages** You must have actually been harmed in a way the law recognizes. This can include:

- Physical injuries
- Medical expenses
- Lost wages
- Property damage
- Pain and suffering
- Emotional distress

Simply being upset or inconvenienced isn't enough - there must be real, measurable harm.

## Real-Life Examples: Negligence in Action

Understanding negligence becomes clearer when you see how it applies to common situations:

### Car Accident Scenario

**The Situation**: Sarah is driving through an intersection when Mike runs a red light and crashes into her car. Sarah suffers a concussion and her car is totaled.

**Breaking Down the Negligence**:

- **Duty**: Mike had a legal duty to follow traffic signals and drive safely
- **Breach**: He breached this duty by running the red light
- **Causation**: His action directly caused the collision and Sarah's injuries
- **Damages**: Sarah has medical bills, car repair costs, and missed work

This is a clear case of negligence, and Sarah would likely have a strong claim for compensation.

## Grocery Store Slip and Fall

**The Situation**: Tom is shopping when he slips on a puddle of water near the produce section that's been there for two hours. He breaks his wrist in the fall.

**Breaking Down the Negligence**:

- **Duty**: The store had a duty to maintain reasonably safe conditions for customers
- **Breach**: They failed to clean up the spill or warn customers about it within a reasonable time
- **Causation**: The unaddressed spill directly caused Tom's fall and injury
- **Damages**: Tom has medical expenses and time off work

The store would likely be found negligent, though the outcome might depend on factors like how obvious the spill was and whether Tom was paying attention.

## Construction Site Injury

**The Situation**: A construction crew fails to properly secure scaffolding, which collapses and injures a pedestrian walking on the adjacent sidewalk.

**Breaking Down the Negligence**:

- **Duty**: The construction company had a duty to follow safety protocols to protect the public
- **Breach**: They failed to properly secure their equipment
- **Causation**: The improperly secured scaffolding directly caused the pedestrian's injuries
- **Damages**: The pedestrian has significant medical expenses and permanent injuries

This would likely result in a successful negligence claim against the construction company.

## When You Share Some Blame: Comparative Fault

Life is rarely black and white, and accidents often involve some degree of shared responsibility. Fortunately, both New York and California have laws that allow you to recover compensation even if you were partially at fault for your own injury.

### How Comparative Fault Works

Both states use what's called "comparative fault" or "comparative negligence." This means:

- Your compensation is reduced by your percentage of fault
- You can still recover money even if you were partially responsible
- The jury or judge determines what percentage of fault belongs to each party

### New York's Pure Comparative Negligence

New York uses "pure" comparative negligence, which means you can recover damages even if you were mostly at fault - even 99% at fault.

**Example**: You're speeding 10 mph over the limit when another driver runs a stop sign and hits you. A jury might find you 20% at fault for speeding and the other driver 80% at fault for running the stop sign. If your total damages are $100,000, you'd recover $80,000 (reduced by your 20% share of fault).

### California's Comparative Fault System

California also uses comparative fault, with some nuances in how fault is distributed among multiple parties.

**Example**: In a three-car accident, the jury might assign fault as follows: Driver A (30%), Driver B (50%), and you (20%). Your recovery would be reduced by your 20% share of fault.

### What This Means for You

Don't assume you can't recover compensation just because you made a mistake or could have been more careful. Even if you were partially responsible, you may still be entitled to significant compensation. An experienced attorney can help evaluate your case and fight to minimize your assigned percentage of fault.

## Strict Liability: When Fault Doesn't Matter

In some situations, the law holds someone responsible for injuries regardless of how careful they were. This is called "strict liability," and it applies in specific circumstances where society has decided that certain activities or products should carry automatic responsibility.

### Product Liability: Defective Products

If you're injured by a defective product, you may not need to prove the manufacturer was careless. You only need to show:

- The product was defectively designed, manufactured, or lacked proper warnings
- You were using it as intended (or in a reasonably foreseeable way)
- The defect caused your injury

**Common Product Liability Cases**:

- Faulty car parts that cause accidents
- Medical devices that malfunction
- Toys with small parts that pose choking hazards
- Appliances that overheat and cause fires
- Medications with dangerous side effects not disclosed in warnings

**Example**: If a ladder collapses while you're using it properly, and investigation shows a manufacturing defect in the locking mechanism, you could have a strict liability claim. You wouldn't need to prove the manufacturer was negligent - just that the defect existed and caused your injury.

### Animal Attacks: Strict Liability Rules

**California Dog Bite Law** California has strict liability for dog bites, meaning dog owners are automatically responsible for injuries their dogs cause, even if:

- The dog has never bitten anyone before
- The owner had no reason to think the dog was dangerous
- The owner took reasonable precautions

**New York Dog Bite Law** New York takes a more limited approach. Strict liability applies only if the dog owner knew or should have known their dog had "vicious propensities." Otherwise, you'd need to prove negligence.

### Other Strict Liability Situations

- **Abnormally dangerous activities**: Using explosives, storing hazardous chemicals
- **Wild animals**: Keeping tigers, bears, or other wild animals as pets
- **Some workplace injuries**: Workers' compensation systems provide strict liability coverage for job-related injuries

## Intentional Torts: When Someone Means to Cause Harm

Sometimes injuries result from deliberate, intentional actions rather than carelessness. These are called "intentional torts," and they're handled differently from negligence cases.

### Common Intentional Torts

#### Assault and Battery

- **Assault**: Making someone reasonably fear they're about to be physically harmed
- **Battery**: Actually making harmful or offensive physical contact
- These often occur together but are legally separate concepts

**False Imprisonment** Illegally restraining someone against their will, such as:

- Locking someone in a room
- Blocking their path when they try to leave
- Detaining someone without legal authority

**Intentional Infliction of Emotional Distress** Extreme and outrageous conduct intended to cause severe emotional suffering. This is a high bar - the conduct must be truly shocking to the average person.

**Defamation (Libel and Slander)**

- **Libel**: Written false statements that damage someone's reputation
- **Slander**: Spoken false statements that damage someone's reputation

### Why Intentional Torts Matter

If someone intentionally harmed you, you may be entitled to:

- **Compensatory damages**: For your actual losses (medical bills, lost wages, pain and suffering)
- **Punitive damages**: Additional money meant to punish the wrongdoer and deter similar conduct

Intentional tort cases often proceed alongside criminal charges, though the civil case (your lawsuit) is separate from any criminal prosecution.

## Building Your Case: What Evidence Matters

Winning a personal injury case requires more than just telling your story - you need evidence that convinces a judge or jury. Here's what typically matters most:

### Types of Evidence

**Witness Testimony**

- People who saw what happened
- Your treating doctors

- Expert witnesses who can explain technical aspects
- Character witnesses (in some cases)

**Physical Evidence**

- Photographs of the accident scene
- Pictures of your injuries
- Damaged property (your car, clothing, etc.)
- The product that caused your injury

**Documentation**

- Police reports
- Medical records and bills
- Employment records showing lost wages
- Insurance correspondence
- Maintenance records (for premises liability cases)

**Electronic Evidence**

- Surveillance camera footage
- Cell phone records (to show someone was texting while driving)
- Social media posts
- GPS data

## The Importance of Acting Quickly

Evidence can disappear quickly:

- Security footage is often erased after 30-90 days
- Witnesses' memories fade
- Physical evidence can be lost or destroyed
- Your own memories may become less clear over time

This is why it's crucial to document everything immediately and consult with an attorney as soon as possible after your injury.

## What Damages Can You Recover?

If you successfully prove your case, you may be entitled to various types of compensation:

### Economic Damages (Quantifiable Losses)

- **Medical expenses**: Hospital bills, doctor visits, medications, physical therapy
- **Future medical costs**: Ongoing treatment, surgeries, medical equipment
- **Lost wages**: Income you've already lost due to your injury
- **Lost earning capacity**: Reduced ability to earn money in the future
- **Property damage**: Repair or replacement costs for damaged belongings

### Non-Economic Damages (Subjective Losses)

- **Pain and suffering**: Physical pain and discomfort
- **Emotional distress**: Anxiety, depression, PTSD
- **Loss of enjoyment of life**: Inability to participate in activities you once enjoyed
- **Disfigurement or scarring**: Permanent changes to your appearance
- **Loss of consortium**: Impact on your relationship with your spouse

### Punitive Damages (Rare)

In cases involving especially reckless or intentional conduct, you might be awarded punitive damages meant to punish the wrongdoer and deter similar behavior.

## Common Challenges and How to Overcome Them

### "It Was Just an Accident"

The other side might argue that what happened was just an unfortunate accident with no one at fault. Your attorney will need to show that reasonable care could have prevented your injury.

### Pre-existing Conditions

If you had health problems before your accident, the defense might claim your current symptoms aren't related to their client's actions. Medical experts can help establish how the incident worsened your pre-existing condition.

### Gaps in Medical Treatment

If you didn't seek immediate medical care or missed appointments, the defense might argue your injuries aren't serious. Always follow your doctor's treatment plan and document any reasons for delays in care.

### Social Media and Surveillance

Be careful about what you post online and assume you might be watched. Photos of you engaging in physical activities could be used to argue your injuries aren't as severe as claimed.

## When to Consult an Attorney

While not every minor injury requires legal representation, you should strongly consider consulting an attorney if:

- Your injuries are serious or require ongoing treatment
- Someone disputes that they were at fault
- Insurance companies are offering inadequate settlements
- Multiple parties might be responsible
- Your injury affects your ability to work

- You're facing significant medical bills
- The incident involved a commercial vehicle, government entity, or dangerous product

Most personal injury attorneys work on a contingency fee basis, meaning you don't pay unless they recover money for you. This makes legal representation accessible even when you're dealing with medical bills and lost income.

## Key Takeaways

Understanding negligence and fault assignment is crucial for protecting your rights after an injury. Remember these important points:

1. **Negligence requires four elements**: duty, breach, causation, and damages - all must be present
2. **You can still recover compensation even if you were partially at fault**
3. **Some situations involve strict liability where fault doesn't matter**
4. **Intentional harm cases are handled differently and may include punitive damages**
5. **Evidence is crucial and can disappear quickly**
6. **Various types of damages may be available beyond just medical bills**

The legal system can seem complex, but these fundamental principles govern most personal injury cases. Whether you're dealing with a car accident, slip and fall, defective product, or intentional harm, understanding these concepts will help you make informed decisions about your case and work effectively with your legal team to seek the compensation you deserve.

Your rights are important, and the law provides pathways to recovery when others' carelessness or intentional actions cause you harm. Don't let confusion about legal concepts prevent you from seeking the justice and compensation you're entitled to receive.

5

# Your Rights After a Personal Injury

*Know What You Are Entitled To*

**When you're hurt, knowing your rights can make the difference between a fair recovery and a devastating financial loss.**

In the immediate aftermath of an injury, most people feel overwhelmed by pain, confusion, and uncertainty. You may be facing a whirlwind of medical appointments, insurance calls, and missed work - all while trying to understand your legal options and rights.

This comprehensive guide will help you navigate those critical early days by clarifying your fundamental rights, outlining essential actions you must take, and identifying common mistakes that can severely undermine your claim's value.

## Your Five Fundamental Rights After an Injury

## Right #1: The Right to Immediate and Comprehensive Medical Care

**Your health comes first, and seeking medical attention is both a right and a strategic necessity.**

Your first and most important right after any injury is to receive prompt and appropriate medical attention. This right exists regardless of:

- Whether you have insurance
- Who caused the accident
- How minor your injuries initially appear
- Your ability to pay upfront

**Why immediate medical care is crucial:**

Even injuries that seem minor at first can escalate into serious medical conditions. Internal injuries, traumatic brain injuries, soft-tissue damage, and psychological trauma often have delayed symptoms that may not appear for hours, days, or even weeks after an incident.

**What "appropriate medical care" means:**

- Emergency room treatment for serious injuries
- Urgent care for moderate injuries that need same-day attention
- Primary care physician evaluation for seemingly minor injuries
- Specialist referrals when recommended by your doctor
- Follow-up appointments and ongoing treatment as prescribed

**Your medical care checklist:**

- Visit a doctor or emergency room immediately after any injury
- Be completely honest about all symptoms, even if they seem unrelated
- Follow all treatment recommendations without skipping appointments
- Keep detailed copies of all medical records, prescriptions, test results, and receipts

- Document any changes in your condition or new symptoms
- Get referrals to specialists when recommended

**Important note:** Medical records serve as crucial evidence if you later pursue a personal injury claim. Insurance companies and opposing counsel will scrutinize your medical treatment timeline, so consistent, thorough documentation is essential.

## Right #2: The Right to Full and Fair Compensation

**If someone else's negligence caused your injury, you have the legal right to pursue complete compensation for all your losses.**

This right exists whether your injury occurred in a car accident, slip and fall, medical malpractice incident, product defect situation, or any other scenario where someone else's negligence harmed you.

**Types of compensation you may be entitled to:**

**Economic damages (quantifiable financial losses):**

- All medical expenses (past, current, and future)
- Lost wages from time missed at work
- Reduced earning capacity if you can't return to your previous job
- Property damage to vehicles, personal belongings, etc.
- Transportation costs to medical appointments
- Home modifications needed due to disability
- Medical equipment and assistive devices

**Non-economic damages (subjective losses):**

- Pain and suffering from physical injuries
- Emotional distress and mental anguish
- Loss of enjoyment of life and activities you can no longer participate in
- Permanent disfigurement or scarring

- Loss of consortium (impact on your relationship with spouse/family)

**Punitive damages (in cases of extreme negligence):**

- Additional compensation designed to punish the wrongdoer
- Only awarded in cases involving particularly reckless or intentional conduct

**How you can pursue compensation:**

- Insurance claim with the at-fault party's insurance company
- Settlement negotiations outside of court
- Formal lawsuit and potential trial
- Workers' compensation claim (for workplace injuries)
- No-fault insurance benefits (in certain states and situations)

**Your right to legal representation:** You have the absolute right to consult with an attorney to assess your potential recovery and develop a legal strategy. Most personal injury attorneys work on a contingency fee basis, meaning you pay nothing unless they recover compensation for you.

## Right #3: The Right to Remain Silent and Avoid Self-Incrimination

**What you say (or don't say) in the aftermath of an injury can significantly impact your claim's value.**

While it's natural to want to explain what happened or express concern for others involved, certain statements - especially apologies - can be misinterpreted as admissions of fault that severely damage your case.

**Statements to avoid at all costs:**

- "I'm sorry" or "It was my fault"
- "I should have been more careful"
- "I didn't see you coming"
- Speculating about what caused the accident
- Minimizing your injuries ("I'm fine" or "It's just a scratch")

**When dealing with insurance adjusters:**

- You are NOT required to give a recorded statement immediately
- You have the right to consult with an attorney before speaking with any insurance company
- You can request that all communications go through your attorney
- Be cautious about signing any documents without legal review

**Social media considerations:** Your social media activity is likely being monitored by insurance companies and opposing counsel. Avoid:

- Posting photos or updates about the incident
- Discussing your injuries or treatment
- Posting images that might contradict your injury claims
- Accepting friend requests from unknown individuals

**What you should say:**

- Stick to basic facts: "The accident happened at [time] at [location]"
- "I need medical attention"
- "I want to contact my attorney"
- "I'll need to review that with my lawyer before I can respond"

## Right #4: The Right to Preserve and Document Evidence

**You have the right to gather and preserve evidence that supports your claim, and others have an obligation not to destroy relevant evidence.**

**Your evidence-gathering rights include:**

- Taking photographs and videos at the accident scene
- Obtaining contact information from witnesses
- Requesting copies of police reports and incident reports
- Accessing your own medical records
- Obtaining security camera footage (before it's automatically deleted)

- Preserving damaged property as evidence

**Steps to protect crucial evidence:**

- Take multiple photos from different angles of the accident scene
- Document vehicle damage, property damage, and visible injuries
- Get names, phone numbers, and insurance information from all parties involved
- Ask witnesses to provide written statements or record brief video testimonials
- Request that relevant surveillance footage be preserved
- Keep all damaged clothing, equipment, or personal items

**Evidence preservation obligations:** Once you've indicated an intention to pursue a claim, the opposing party has a legal obligation to preserve relevant evidence. This includes:

- Surveillance footage
- Maintenance records
- Employee training records
- Internal communications
- Physical evidence

## Right #5: The Right to Fair Treatment by Insurance Companies

**Insurance companies must handle your claim in good faith and cannot unreasonably delay, deny, or undervalue legitimate claims.**

**Your rights when dealing with insurers:**

- The right to have your claim investigated promptly and thoroughly
- The right to receive a reasonable settlement offer based on the evidence
- The right to understand why a claim was denied

- The right to appeal denied claims
- Protection from bad faith insurance practices

**Common bad faith insurance tactics to watch for:**

- Unreasonable delays in processing your claim
- Requesting excessive or irrelevant documentation
- Offering settlements far below your claim's actual value
- Misrepresenting policy language or coverage
- Failing to conduct a proper investigation

## Critical Actions You Must Take Immediately

### The First 24 Hours

**Seek medical attention** Even if you feel "fine," adrenaline and shock can mask serious injuries. Get evaluated by a medical professional.

**Document everything** Take photos, gather witness information, and create a written account of what happened while details are fresh in your memory.

**Report the incident** File necessary reports with police, employers, property owners, or other relevant parties.

**Contact your insurance company** Report the incident to your own insurance company, even if you weren't at fault.

### The First Week

**Follow up with medical care** Attend all scheduled appointments and follow treatment recommendations precisely.

**Organize your documentation** Create a file system for medical records, insurance correspondence, receipts, and other claim-related documents.

**Consider legal consultation** Speak with a personal injury attorney to understand your rights and options.

**Be cautious with communications** Limit what you say to insurance adjusters and avoid giving recorded statements without legal counsel.

## Common Mistakes That Can Destroy Your Claim's Value

### Mistake #1: Delaying Medical Treatment

**Why this hurts your case:** Insurance companies argue that delayed treatment means either:

- Your injuries weren't serious
- Your injuries were caused by something other than the incident
- You're exaggerating your symptoms

**How to avoid this mistake:**

- Seek medical attention within 24 hours of any injury
- If you initially declined medical treatment, seek care as soon as symptoms appear
- Keep detailed records of how you felt each day after the incident

### Mistake #2: Failing to Document the Scene and Your Injuries

**Why documentation matters:** Without proper documentation, it becomes your word against theirs. Photos, videos, and witness statements provide objective evidence of what happened.

**What to document:**

- The accident scene from multiple angles
- All vehicle damage or property damage
- Visible injuries (bruises, cuts, swelling)
- Weather and lighting conditions
- Any relevant signage or road conditions

- Your injuries as they develop and heal

## Mistake #3: Trusting Insurance Adjusters

**Remember: Insurance adjusters work for the insurance company, not for you.**

Their job is to settle claims for as little money as possible. Common adjuster tactics include:

- Pressuring you to settle quickly before you know the full extent of your injuries
- Asking leading questions designed to get you to admit fault
- Requesting excessive documentation to delay your claim
- Making lowball settlement offers hoping you'll accept out of desperation

**How to protect yourself:**

- Never give a recorded statement without consulting an attorney
- Don't sign anything without legal review
- Document all communications with adjusters
- Remember that their first offer is rarely their best offer

## Mistake #4: Inconsistent Medical Treatment

**Why treatment consistency matters:** Gaps in treatment or missed appointments can be interpreted as evidence that you're not actually injured or that you're not following medical advice.

**How to maintain consistent treatment:**

- Attend every scheduled appointment
- If you must reschedule, do so promptly and document the reason
- Follow all treatment recommendations, even if you're feeling better
- Communicate openly with your healthcare providers about your symptoms and progress

### Mistake #5: Providing Too Much Information Too Soon

**The problem with over-sharing:** In your eagerness to be helpful and honest, you might inadvertently say something that damages your case.

**Better approach:**

- Stick to basic facts
- Avoid speculation about what caused the accident
- Don't discuss your injuries in detail until you've consulted with an attorney
- Let your lawyer handle communications with insurance companies

## State-Specific Rights and Protections

### New York Rights and Protections

**No-Fault Insurance Benefits** New York's no-fault insurance law provides important protections:

- You're entitled to no-fault benefits through your own insurance policy after a car accident, regardless of who caused the crash
- Benefits include up to $50,000 in medical expenses, lost earnings up to $2,000 per month, and other necessary costs
- You can access these benefits immediately without proving fault

**Serious Injury Threshold** To sue for pain and suffering in New York, your injury must meet the state's "serious injury" threshold:

- Death
- Dismemberment
- Significant disfigurement
- Fracture
- Loss of a fetus
- Permanent loss of use of a body organ, member, function or system

- Permanent consequential limitation of use of a body organ or member
- Significant limitation of use of a body function or system
- Medically determined injury or impairment of a non-permanent nature which prevents the injured person from performing substantially all of the material acts which constitute such person's usual and customary daily activities for not less than 90 days during the 180 days immediately following the occurrence of the injury or impairment

**Statute of Limitations**

- Personal injury claims: 3 years from the date of injury
- Medical malpractice: 2.5 years from the date of malpractice
- Wrongful death: 2 years from the date of death

## California Rights and Protections

**Pure Comparative Fault System** California's comparative fault law is particularly favorable to injured parties:

- You can recover compensation even if you were partially at fault for the accident
- Your compensation will be reduced by your percentage of fault, but not eliminated
- For example, if you're found 30% at fault, you can still recover 70% of your total damages

**No Damage Caps** Unlike many states, California generally doesn't cap damages in personal injury cases, meaning you can potentially recover full compensation for all your losses.

**Statute of Limitations**

- Personal injury claims: 2 years from the date of injury
- Property damage: 3 years from the date of damage
- Medical malpractice: 3 years from the date of discovery or 1 year from when you should have reasonably discovered the malpractice

## When You Absolutely Need an Attorney

While you're not legally required to hire an attorney for every injury claim, certain situations make legal representation essential:

### Complex Cases Requiring Legal Expertise

**Serious or permanent injuries**

- Injuries requiring surgery or long-term treatment
- Permanent disability or disfigurement
- Traumatic brain injuries
- Spinal cord injuries

**Disputed liability**

- When fault is unclear or contested
- Multiple parties may be responsible
- Accidents involving commercial vehicles or businesses

**Insurance complications**

- Claim denials or delays
- Bad faith insurance practices
- Insufficient insurance coverage
- Multiple insurance policies involved

### Financial Considerations

**High-value claims** When significant money is at stake, the insurance company will have experienced attorneys and adjusters working to minimize their payout. You need equal representation.

**Lost income implications** If your injury affects your ability to work, an attorney can help calculate and prove future lost earnings, including:

- Reduced earning capacity

- Lost advancement opportunities
- Benefits and pension losses

### Legal Complexity

**Statute of limitations concerns** Each state has strict deadlines for filing personal injury claims. Missing these deadlines means losing your right to compensation forever.

**Evidence preservation** Attorneys know how to quickly preserve crucial evidence before it's lost or destroyed.

**Medical documentation** Lawyers work with medical experts to properly document and present your injuries' full impact.

## What to Look for in a Personal Injury Attorney

### Experience and Specialization

- Look for attorneys who specialize in personal injury law
- Ask about their experience with cases similar to yours
- Inquire about their trial experience (many cases settle, but you want an attorney prepared to go to court)

### Resources and Support

- Does the firm have the resources to properly investigate and develop your case?
- Do they work with medical experts, accident reconstruction specialists, and other professionals?
- Can they advance case expenses if needed?

### Communication and Accessibility

- Will you work directly with the attorney or mainly with support staff?
- How quickly do they respond to phone calls and emails?

- Do they explain legal concepts in terms you can understand?

### Fee Structure

- Most personal injury attorneys work on contingency fees (typically 33-40% of any recovery)
- Make sure you understand what expenses you'll be responsible for
- Get the fee agreement in writing

## Your Action Plan: Next Steps

### Immediate Actions (First 24-48 Hours)

1. **Seek medical attention** - Even for seemingly minor injuries
2. **Document everything** - Photos, witness information, your account of events
3. **Report the incident** - To police, employers, property owners as appropriate
4. **Contact your insurance** - Report to your own insurance company
5. **Preserve evidence** - Keep damaged items, clothing, etc.

### Short-term Actions (First 1-2 Weeks)

1. **Organize documentation** - Create a system for all claim-related paperwork
2. **Follow medical treatment** - Attend all appointments and follow recommendations
3. **Research attorneys** - If your case involves serious injuries or disputed fault
4. **Limit communications** - Be cautious about what you say to insurance adjusters
5. **Document your recovery** - Keep a daily journal of symptoms and limitations

### Ongoing Actions

1. **Maintain consistent medical treatment** - Don't skip appointments or stop treatment prematurely
2. **Keep detailed records** - All expenses, lost wages, and how injuries affect your daily life
3. **Follow your attorney's advice** - If you've hired legal representation
4. **Be patient** - Personal injury claims take time to develop and resolve properly

## Final Thoughts: Protecting Your Future

Being injured due to someone else's negligence is stressful enough without worrying about whether you're protecting your legal rights. By understanding your fundamental rights, taking prompt action, and avoiding common mistakes, you can maximize your chances of a fair recovery.

Remember that insurance companies have teams of experienced professionals working to minimize what they pay you. Don't try to navigate this process alone, especially when serious injuries or significant money are involved. Your future financial security and quality of life may depend on the decisions you make in the days and weeks following your injury.

The most important takeaway: **Act quickly, document everything, seek appropriate medical care, and don't hesitate to consult with a qualified personal injury attorney who can protect your rights and maximize your recovery.**

Your recovery - both physical and financial - depends on the actions you take right now. Don't let this opportunity slip away.

# 6

# First Steps After the Injury

## *Your First Moves to Protect Yourself*

The moments after an injury can feel overwhelming and chaotic. You might be in pain, confused, or dealing with shock. However, the actions you take in these crucial first hours and days will significantly impact both your recovery and any potential legal claim. This guide walks you through exactly what to do, step by step, to protect your health, your rights, and your financial future.

### Why These First Steps Matter So Much

When you're injured due to someone else's negligence, you're not just dealing with physical pain - you're entering a complex world of insurance claims, legal procedures, and documentation requirements. Insurance companies and opposing parties will immediately begin building their defense, often within hours of an incident. The evidence you preserve and the actions you take now will determine whether you can successfully recover compensation for your medical bills, lost wages, pain and suffering, and other damages.

**Remember: Insurance companies are not on your side.** Their goal is to minimize payouts, and they'll use any gaps in documentation, delays in medical treatment, or inconsistent statements against you.

## Step 1: Prioritize Safety and Get Medical Help

### Immediate Safety First

- **Move to safety** if you can do so without worsening injuries
- **Call 911** if anyone appears seriously injured or if you're unsure about the severity
- **Turn on hazard lights** in vehicle accidents
- **Check on others** involved but avoid moving anyone who might have spinal injuries

### Seek Medical Attention - Even If You Feel "Fine"

This is perhaps the most critical step, and here's why:

**Adrenaline masks pain.** After an accident, your body releases adrenaline and endorphins that can hide serious injuries. You might feel fine initially but develop severe pain hours or days later.

**Insurance companies scrutinize treatment delays.** If you wait weeks to see a doctor, insurers will argue your injuries weren't caused by the accident or aren't as serious as you claim.

**Some injuries have delayed symptoms:**

- Concussions and traumatic brain injuries
- Herniated discs and spinal injuries
- Internal bleeding
- Soft tissue injuries like whiplash
- Psychological trauma and PTSD

### What to Tell Medical Professionals

- Describe **all** areas of discomfort, even minor ones
- Mention the accident and how it occurred

- Be honest about pre-existing conditions - hiding them can hurt your case later
- Ask for copies of all medical records and reports

**Pro Tip:** Go to an emergency room or urgent care, not just your family doctor. ER visits create immediate documentation linking your injuries to the accident.

## Step 2: Document Everything Like Your Case Depends on It (Because It Does)

Evidence disappears quickly. Skid marks fade, debris gets cleaned up, witnesses leave, and people's memories become less reliable. You need to act fast and be thorough.

### Photography and Video Documentation

**Take photos of everything, even if it seems unimportant:**

**For Vehicle Accidents:**

- All vehicles from multiple angles
- License plates of all vehicles involved
- Damage to your vehicle (close-ups and wide shots)
- The accident scene, including road conditions
- Traffic signs, signals, or construction zones
- Skid marks, debris, or broken glass
- Your injuries (if visible)
- Inside your vehicle showing airbag deployment, broken glass, etc.

**For Slip and Fall Accidents:**

- The exact spot where you fell
- What caused you to fall (wet floor, broken step, debris)
- Lack of warning signs

- Poor lighting conditions
- Your injuries
- Your torn or damaged clothing
- The surrounding area showing context

**For Product Liability Cases:**

- The defective product from all angles
- Serial numbers, model numbers, or identifying marks
- Instructions or warning labels
- Where you purchased it (receipt if available)
- How the product failed or malfunctioned

## Environmental and Situational Documentation

Record details about:

- **Weather conditions** (rain, snow, fog affecting visibility)
- **Time of day** and lighting conditions
- **Road or floor surfaces** (wet, icy, uneven, poorly maintained)
- **Visibility factors** (sun glare, broken streetlights)
- **Construction zones** or temporary hazards
- **Your activities** immediately before the incident

## Preserve Physical Evidence

Keep everything in a safe place:

- Damaged clothing or personal items
- Defective products or parts that broke
- Medical devices like crutches or braces
- Anything else connected to your accident

**Important:** Don't repair or throw away damaged items until you've consulted with an attorney.

## Step 3: Gather Witness Information Immediately

Witnesses can make or break your case. Their independent accounts of what happened provide crucial third-party verification of your version of events.

### What Information to Collect

For each witness, get:

- **Full name** (ask to see ID if needed)
- **Phone number** (cell and home if available)
- **Email address**
- **Home or work address**
- **Brief description** of what they saw
- **Ask them to write a statement** if they're willing

### How to Approach Witnesses

- Be polite and explain you were in an accident
- Ask if they saw what happened
- If they seem helpful, ask for their contact information
- Don't coach them or suggest what they should have seen
- Thank them for their time

### Special Witness Situations

**Security Cameras:** If the incident occurred at a business, ask about security footage immediately. Many systems automatically delete footage after 30-90 days.

**Traffic Cameras:** Note if there are red light cameras or traffic monitoring devices that might have captured the accident.

**Dashcam Footage:** Ask other drivers if they have dashcam footage of the incident.

## Step 4: File Required Reports and Create Official Records

Official reports create permanent records of your accident that insurance companies and courts will rely on. Missing deadlines or failing to report can seriously damage your case.

### Motor Vehicle Accidents

**Police Reports:**

- Call police even for "minor" accidents - what seems minor now might not be later
- When officers arrive, stick to facts and avoid speculation
- Don't admit fault, even if you think you might be partially responsible
- Get the officer's name and report number
- Ask how to obtain a copy of the report (usually available 3-7 days later)

**Insurance Reporting:**

- **Your insurance company:** Report the accident immediately, even if the other driver was at fault
- **Other driver's insurance:** You'll typically report this later, often through your attorney
- **Provide facts only:** Don't speculate about fault or injuries

### Workplace Injuries

**Immediate Reporting:**

- Notify your supervisor **immediately**, even for minor injuries
- Follow your company's accident reporting procedures exactly

- Ask for copies of all forms you complete
- Don't let your employer pressure you to avoid filing a report

**Workers' Compensation Claims:**

- File your workers' comp claim promptly (deadlines vary by state)
- Keep copies of all paperwork
- Attend all required medical appointments
- Don't sign any documents without understanding them fully

### Premises Liability (Slip and Fall, etc.)

**Business/Property Owner Notification:**

- Report the incident to a manager or owner immediately
- Ask them to create an incident report
- Request a copy of the report
- Get the manager's name and contact information
- Take photos of any "wet floor" signs put up after your fall

## Step 5: Protect Yourself from Damaging Statements

In the stress and confusion after an accident, it's natural to want to be polite and helpful. However, certain phrases can be twisted and used against you later.

### What NOT to Say

**Never say "I'm sorry"** - Even if you're just being polite, "I'm sorry" can be interpreted as an admission of guilt.

**Don't speculate about cause** - Phrases like "I didn't see the stop sign" or "I was probably going too fast" can destroy your case.

**Avoid minimizing injuries** - Don't say "I'm fine" or "It's just a scratch" even if you think that's true. You might discover serious injuries later.

**Don't discuss fault** - Let the investigation determine who was responsible.

## What TO Say Instead

- "I need medical attention"
- "Let's wait for the police to determine what happened"
- "I'd like to report this incident"
- "I'll need to speak with my insurance company/attorney before giving a detailed statement"

## Dealing with Insurance Adjusters

**Your Own Insurance Company:**

- Report the claim promptly
- Provide basic facts about what happened
- Be honest but don't speculate

**Other Party's Insurance:**

- You're not required to give them a statement immediately
- It's often best to say: "I'm still receiving medical treatment and would prefer to discuss this through my attorney"
- **Never accept a quick settlement offer** without legal advice

**Recorded Statements:**

- Insurance companies often request recorded statements within days of an accident
- You have the right to decline or postpone these
- If you do give one, stick to basic facts and don't speculate

# Step 6: Track Every Expense and Impact

Your compensation depends on proving your damages. Start documenting costs and impacts immediately, even for seemingly small expenses.

## Medical Expenses to Track

- **Emergency room visits**
- **Doctor appointments** (including co-pays)
- **Specialist consultations**
- **Physical therapy sessions**
- **Prescription medications**
- **Medical equipment** (crutches, braces, wheelchairs)
- **Home health care**
- **Future medical costs** (get estimates from doctors)

## Lost Income Documentation

- **Missed work days** (keep a calendar)
- **Hourly wages or salary information**
- **Lost overtime opportunities**
- **Missed bonuses or commissions**
- **Used sick days or vacation time**
- **Reduced earning capacity** if you can't perform your job the same way

## Transportation and Other Expenses

- **Gas money** for medical appointments
- **Parking fees** at hospitals/clinics
- **Public transportation costs**
- **Rideshare or taxi expenses**
- **Childcare costs** if you can't care for your children
- **Home modifications** (ramps, grab bars, etc.)

### Pain and Suffering Documentation

Keep a daily journal documenting:

- **Pain levels** (rate 1-10 each day)
- **Activities you can't do** anymore
- **Sleep problems**
- **Emotional impacts** (depression, anxiety, frustration)
- **How injuries affect your relationships**
- **Missed family events or social activities**

### Organization Tips

- **Create a dedicated file folder** (physical and digital)
- **Scan all receipts** and store digitally
- **Take photos** of receipts that might fade
- **Use a spreadsheet** to track expenses by category
- **Keep a separate bank account** for injury-related expenses if possible

## Step 7: Know When You Need an Attorney

Not every injury requires an attorney, but many situations are too complex or valuable to handle alone. Here's when you should strongly consider legal representation:

### Definitely Consult an Attorney If:

**Serious Injuries:**

- Broken bones
- Head or brain injuries
- Spinal cord injuries
- Injuries requiring surgery

- Permanent disability or disfigurement
- Injuries affecting your ability to work

**Complex Liability:**

- Multiple parties involved
- Disputes about who was at fault
- Government entities involved
- Defective products caused your injury

**Insurance Problems:**

- Your claim is denied
- Offered settlement seems too low
- Insurance company is delaying your claim
- Multiple insurance companies are involved

**Significant Financial Impact:**

- Medical bills exceed $10,000
- You've missed substantial work time
- You have ongoing medical needs
- Your future earning capacity is affected

## What an Attorney Can Do for You

**Evidence Preservation:**

- Send preservation letters to prevent destruction of evidence
- Hire accident reconstruction experts
- Interview witnesses professionally
- Obtain security footage before it's deleted

**Medical Case Building:**

- Connect you with appropriate specialists

- Ensure you get all necessary treatment
- Obtain proper medical documentation
- Calculate future medical costs

**Insurance Negotiations:**

- Handle all communications with insurance companies
- Calculate the true value of your claim
- Negotiate for maximum compensation
- Protect you from unfair settlement tactics

**Legal Procedures:**

- File lawsuits within statute of limitations deadlines
- Handle complex legal paperwork
- Represent you in court if necessary
- Navigate court procedures and rules

## How to Choose the Right Attorney

**Look for:**

- Specialization in personal injury law
- Experience with cases similar to yours
- Good track record of settlements and verdicts
- Clear communication style
- Willingness to take your case to trial if needed

**Questions to Ask:**

- How many cases like mine have you handled?
- What's your success rate?
- How do you communicate with clients?
- What are your fees? (Most personal injury attorneys work on

contingency)

- Who will actually work on my case?

## State-Specific Requirements: New York vs. California

### New York Specific Rules

**No-Fault Insurance:**

- New York requires no-fault auto insurance
- Your own insurance pays medical bills and lost wages up to policy limits, regardless of fault
- You must notify your insurance company immediately to preserve no-fault benefits
- You can only sue the at-fault driver for pain and suffering if you meet the "serious injury threshold"

**Municipal Claims:**

- If a government entity (city, county, state) caused your injury, you must file a **Notice of Claim within 90 days**
- This is a strict deadline with very few exceptions
- The notice must include specific information about your claim
- Missing this deadline usually bars your claim entirely

**Statute of Limitations:**

- Personal injury claims: 3 years from the date of injury
- Medical malpractice: 2.5 years from the date of malpractice
- Product liability: 3 years from injury discovery

### California Specific Rules

**At-Fault System:**

- California uses a pure comparative fault system
- You can recover damages even if you're partially at fault
- Your compensation is reduced by your percentage of fault
- This makes documentation of the other party's negligence crucial

**Government Claims:**

- Claims against public agencies must be filed **within 6 months** of the incident
- This includes claims against cities, counties, state agencies, and school districts
- The claim must be submitted to the appropriate government entity
- If denied, you have 6 months to file a lawsuit

**Statute of Limitations:**

- Personal injury claims: 2 years from the date of injury
- Medical malpractice: 3 years from injury discovery or 1 year from when you should have discovered it
- Product liability: 2 years from injury discovery

**Proposition 213 Impact:**

- If you were uninsured at the time of an auto accident, you cannot recover non-economic damages (pain and suffering) from other drivers
- This applies even if the other driver was 100% at fault
- Economic damages (medical bills, lost wages) are still recoverable

## Red Flags: When Insurance Companies Are Playing Games

Insurance companies often use tactics to minimize or deny valid claims. Watch out for these warning signs:

### Delay Tactics

- Taking weeks to return phone calls
- Repeatedly asking for the same documentation
- Claiming they need to "investigate further" without explanation
- Missing deadlines for claim processing

### Low-Ball Settlement Offers

- Quick settlement offers within days of your accident
- Offers that don't cover your medical bills
- Pressure to settle before you know the full extent of your injuries
- Claims that their offer is "final" when it's not

### Denial Strategies

- Claiming you were at fault without proper investigation
- Arguing your injuries weren't caused by the accident
- Disputing the necessity of your medical treatment
- Using pre-existing conditions to deny your entire claim

### Investigation Misconduct

- Hiring investigators to follow you and take video
- Demanding excessive medical records
- Questioning your doctors inappropriately
- Misrepresenting facts in their investigation

**If you encounter any of these tactics, it's time to consult an attorney immediately.**

## Special Situations: Additional Considerations

### Accidents Involving Commercial Vehicles

**Trucking Accidents:**

- Commercial trucks have higher insurance coverage
- Federal regulations may apply
- Multiple parties might be liable (driver, trucking company, cargo loader)
- Electronic logging devices provide valuable evidence
- Special accident reconstruction may be needed

**Rideshare Accidents (Uber/Lyft):**

- Coverage depends on whether driver was logged into the app
- Multiple insurance policies might apply
- Complex liability issues between rideshare company and driver
- Document whether the driver was on duty at the time

## Product Liability Claims

**When Products Cause Injury:**

- Keep the defective product in a safe place
- Don't attempt repairs or modifications
- Document how you were using the product when it failed
- Keep all packaging, instructions, and receipts
- Note where and when you purchased the product

## Accidents Involving Minors

**Special Protections for Children:**

- Longer statute of limitations periods
- Courts must approve settlements
- Special consideration for future impacts

- Different standards for determining fault

### Dog Bite Cases

**Immediate Actions:**

- Get medical attention immediately (infection risk is high)
- Identify the dog's owner
- Determine vaccination status
- Report to animal control
- Document all injuries with photos
- Get witness information

## Building Your Support Network

Recovery from a personal injury affects every aspect of your life. Building a strong support network helps both your recovery and your legal case.

### Medical Team

- **Primary care physician** for ongoing care coordination
- **Specialists** as recommended (orthopedists, neurologists, etc.)
- **Physical therapists** for rehabilitation
- **Mental health professionals** for emotional impacts
- **Pain management specialists** if needed

### Legal Team

- **Personal injury attorney** as your primary advocate
- **Legal assistants/paralegals** who handle day-to-day communications
- **Expert witnesses** (accident reconstructionists, medical experts, economists)

### Personal Support

- **Family and friends** for emotional support
- **Support groups** for people with similar injuries
- **Social workers** to help navigate systems and benefits
- **Financial advisors** for long-term planning if disability is permanent

## Technology Tools to Help Your Case

### Smartphone Apps

- **Voice recording apps** for documenting daily symptoms
- **Photo organization apps** to categorize evidence photos
- **Expense tracking apps** to monitor injury-related costs
- **Calendar apps** to track medical appointments and missed work
- **Navigation apps** that might have location data from the accident

### Cloud Storage

- **Backup all documentation** to prevent loss
- **Share access** with your attorney's office
- **Organize files** by category (medical, financial, legal, photos)

### Wearable Devices

- **Fitness trackers** might show impact of injuries on activity levels
- **Sleep monitors** can document sleep disruption
- **Heart rate monitors** might show stress or pain impacts

## Common Mistakes That Can Ruin Your Case

### Mistake 1: Waiting Too Long to See a Doctor

**Why it's harmful:** Insurance companies argue that delayed treatment means you weren't really injured. **Better approach:** See a medical professional within 24-48 hours, even if you feel okay.

### Mistake 2: Not Following Medical Advice

**Why it's harmful:** Missing appointments or not following treatment plans gives insurers ammunition to claim you're not really injured. **Better approach:** Attend all appointments, follow all treatment recommendations, and document any barriers to treatment.

### Mistake 3: Posting on Social Media

**Why it's harmful:** Photos of you looking happy or active can be taken out of context and used against you. **Better approach:** Avoid posting anything about your accident, injuries, or activities until your case is resolved.

### Mistake 4: Accepting Quick Settlement Offers

**Why it's harmful:** You might not know the full extent of your injuries or future medical needs. **Better approach:**Don't accept any settlement until you've reached maximum medical improvement and consulted an attorney.

### Mistake 5: Talking to the Other Side's Insurance Company

**Why it's harmful:** They're trained to get you to say things that hurt your case. **Better approach:** Refer them to your attorney or politely decline to give detailed statements.

### Mistake 6: Not Keeping Good Records

**Why it's harmful:** Poor documentation makes it difficult to prove your damages. **Better approach:** Document everything from day one and stay organized.

## Recovery Timeline: What to Expect

Understanding the typical timeline helps set realistic expectations and ensures you don't miss critical deadlines.

## Immediate Phase (First 72 Hours)

- Seek emergency medical care
- Document the accident scene
- File necessary reports
- Begin expense tracking
- Contact your insurance company

## Short-term Phase (First 2-4 Weeks)

- Follow up medical care
- Consult with an attorney if needed
- Gather all documentation
- Begin treatment plan
- Handle immediate financial needs

## Medium-term Phase (1-6 Months)

- Continue medical treatment
- Physical therapy and rehabilitation
- Return to work discussions
- Insurance negotiations begin
- Case investigation and evidence gathering

## Long-term Phase (6 Months - 2+ Years)

- Reach maximum medical improvement
- Determine permanent impacts

- Negotiate settlements or prepare for trial
- Resolution of legal claims
- Long-term life adjustments

## Your Action Checklist

Print this checklist and keep it in your car, workplace, and home for quick reference:

### Immediate Actions (First Hour)

- [ ] Ensure safety and call 911 if needed
- [ ] Seek medical attention
- [ ] Take photos/videos of everything
- [ ] Get witness contact information
- [ ] Call police if required
- [ ] Contact your insurance company

### First 24 Hours

- [ ] See a doctor even if you feel fine
- [ ] Create a file for all accident-related documents
- [ ] Start an expense log
- [ ] Write down everything you remember about the accident
- [ ] Research personal injury attorneys if injuries are serious

### First Week

- [ ] Follow up with medical care
- [ ] Obtain police report
- [ ] Organize all documentation

- [ ] Consult with an attorney if needed
- [ ] Begin keeping a daily symptom diary

### Ongoing

- [ ] Attend all medical appointments
- [ ] Keep all receipts and records organized
- [ ] Follow attorney's advice
- [ ] Avoid social media posts about your case
- [ ] Focus on your recovery

## Final Thoughts: Your Recovery Comes First

While protecting your legal rights is important, your primary focus should always be on your physical and emotional recovery. The steps outlined in this guide will help ensure you have the documentation and evidence needed to pursue fair compensation, but don't let the legal process interfere with getting the medical care and support you need.

Remember that every personal injury case is unique. The specific steps you need to take may vary depending on the type of accident, the severity of your injuries, and the laws in your state. When in doubt, consult with a qualified personal injury attorney who can provide guidance tailored to your specific situation.

Most importantly, be patient with yourself. Recovery takes time, and the legal process can be lengthy. Focus on getting better, follow the advice of your medical team, and trust your legal team to handle the complex aspects of your claim.

Your injury doesn't define you, but how you handle the aftermath can significantly impact your future quality of life and financial security. By taking the right steps now, you're giving yourself the best possible chance for a full recovery and fair compensation for your losses.

7

# Medical Treatment and Recordkeeping

*How to Save the Proofs You'll Need Later*

When you're injured due to someone else's negligence, your medical records become the most powerful evidence in your case. They tell the story of your injuries, document your pain and suffering, and prove the financial impact of the incident. This comprehensive guide will help you navigate the medical treatment process while building a strong foundation for your legal claim.

## Why Medical Documentation Can Make or Break Your Case

**Your medical records are your evidence.** Courts, insurance companies, and attorneys all rely on medical documentation to understand:

- The severity and extent of your injuries
- How the incident caused your medical condition
- The treatment you required and its cost

- How your injuries affect your daily life
- Your prognosis and future medical needs

Without proper medical documentation, even legitimate injuries can be questioned, reduced, or denied by insurance companies. A well-documented medical history, on the other hand, can significantly increase your settlement value and strengthen your negotiating position.

## Step 1: Seek Immediate Medical Attention

### The 24-Hour Rule

**See a doctor within 24 hours of your injury, even if you feel fine.** Here's why this timing matters:

- **Adrenaline masks pain:** Your body's natural response to trauma can hide symptoms for hours or even days
- **Some injuries develop gradually:** Whiplash, concussions, and soft tissue injuries often worsen over time
- **Insurance companies look for gaps:** Delays in treatment give insurers ammunition to argue your injuries aren't serious or weren't caused by the incident

### What to Tell Your Doctor

**Be completely honest and thorough** when describing your symptoms. Include:

- **Every area of pain or discomfort** (even if it seems minor)
- **All symptoms** you're experiencing (headaches, dizziness, sleep problems, mood changes)
- **How the injury affects your daily activities** (work, exercise, household tasks, relationships)
- **The exact details of how the injury occurred**

**Important:** Don't downplay your symptoms or say you're "fine" out of politeness. Your medical records should reflect the true impact of your injuries.

### Where to Seek Treatment

**Emergency Room:** Go immediately if you have:

- Severe pain
- Loss of consciousness
- Suspected broken bones
- Head injuries
- Difficulty breathing
- Any life-threatening symptoms

**Urgent Care:** Appropriate for:

- Moderate injuries that need prompt attention
- When your primary doctor isn't available
- Non-life-threatening injuries that shouldn't wait for a regular appointment

**Primary Care Physician:** Best for:

- Follow-up care after emergency treatment
- Ongoing monitoring of your condition
- Referrals to specialists

## Step 2: Follow Your Treatment Plan Religiously

### The Importance of Compliance

Insurance companies scrutinize your treatment compliance. Failing to follow your doctor's orders can be used against you to argue that:

- Your injuries aren't as serious as claimed
- You failed to mitigate your damages
- Your current condition is due to non-compliance, not the original injury

## Key Treatment Components to Follow

**Medical Appointments:**

- Attend every scheduled appointment
- Don't cancel unless absolutely necessary
- If you must reschedule, do so promptly
- Arrive on time and prepared

**Medications:**

- Take all prescribed medications as directed
- Don't stop taking medication without consulting your doctor
- Keep all prescription bottles and receipts
- Report any side effects or concerns

**Physical Therapy:**

- Attend all sessions
- Actively participate in exercises
- Follow home exercise programs
- Communicate with your therapist about progress and setbacks

**Activity Restrictions:**

- Follow work limitations exactly
- Avoid restricted activities (lifting, driving, sports)
- Don't return to work or activities early without medical clearance

## When You Can't Follow Treatment

If financial constraints, transportation issues, or other legitimate barriers prevent you from following treatment, document these challenges:

- Communicate with your healthcare provider about barriers

- Ask about alternative treatment options
- Keep records of why you couldn't comply
- Work with your attorney to address these issues

## Step 3: Build Comprehensive Medical Records

### Essential Medical Documents to Collect

**Primary Treatment Records:**

- Initial emergency room reports
- Doctor's notes from every visit
- Diagnostic test results (X-rays, MRIs, CT scans, blood tests)
- Surgical reports and operative notes
- Hospital discharge summaries
- Physical therapy evaluation and progress notes

**Prescription Documentation:**

- All prescription bottles with labels
- Pharmacy receipts
- Over-the-counter medication receipts
- Medical device receipts (braces, crutches, etc.)

**Specialist Records:**

- Orthopedic evaluations
- Neurological assessments
- Pain management consultations
- Psychological or psychiatric evaluations
- Occupational therapy notes

**Work-Related Documentation:**

- Work restriction letters
- Disability determinations
- Return-to-work evaluations
- Vocational rehabilitation reports

## How to Obtain Your Medical Records

**Request Records Promptly:**

- Contact the medical records department at each facility
- Submit written requests (most facilities have forms)
- Pay any required copying fees
- Follow up if records don't arrive within the stated timeframe

**What to Request:**

- Complete medical records (not just summaries)
- All diagnostic images on CD/DVD
- Laboratory results
- Billing records
- Correspondence between providers

**Tips for Success:**

- Keep copies of all requests
- Request records every few months to stay current
- Ask for records in digital format when possible
- Verify you've received complete files

# Step 4: Document Your Daily Experience

## Keeping a Personal Injury Journal

Your medical records capture the clinical picture, but a personal journal documents the human impact of your injuries. This subjective evidence can be extremely powerful in settlement negotiations.

**What to Record Daily:**

**Pain Levels:**

- Rate pain on a scale of 1-10
- Describe the type of pain (sharp, throbbing, burning)
- Note which activities increase or decrease pain
- Track pain patterns throughout the day

**Functional Limitations:**

- Activities you can no longer perform
- Tasks that are now difficult or painful
- How long you can sit, stand, or walk
- Sleep disruptions

**Emotional Impact:**

- Frustration, anxiety, or depression
- Impact on relationships
- Loss of enjoyment in activities
- Stress from financial concerns

**Work Impact:**

- Days missed from work
- Reduced productivity
- Difficulty with specific job tasks
- Career concerns or limitations

## Sample Journal Entry Format

**Date:** [Date] **Pain Level:** [1-10 scale] **Sleep Quality:** [Hours slept, disruptions] **Activities Attempted:** [What you tried to do] **Limitations Experienced:** [What you couldn't do or had difficulty with] **Emotional State:** [How you felt physically and emotionally] **Medications Taken:** [What and when] **Notes:** [Any other relevant observations]

## Step 5: Organize Your Medical Bills and Financial Records

### Understanding the Financial Impact

Medical bills serve as concrete proof of your economic damages. Proper organization helps ensure you're fully compensated for:

- Past medical expenses
- Ongoing treatment costs
- Future medical needs
- Lost wages due to medical appointments

### Types of Financial Records to Collect

**Direct Medical Costs:**

- Hospital bills (itemized)
- Doctor visit charges
- Diagnostic test fees
- Surgery and anesthesia costs
- Physical therapy charges
- Prescription costs
- Medical device expenses

**Insurance-Related Documents:**

- Insurance Explanation of Benefits (EOB) statements
- Denial letters

- Pre-authorization forms
- Coverage determination letters

**Out-of-Pocket Expenses:**

- Co-payment receipts
- Deductible payments
- Transportation costs to medical appointments
- Parking fees at medical facilities
- Over-the-counter medication receipts

**Lost Income Documentation:**

- Pay stubs showing missed work
- Documentation of used sick/vacation time
- Employer statements about time missed
- Tax returns showing income loss

## Creating an Organized System

**Physical Organization:**

- Use a dedicated filing system with clearly labeled folders
- Separate folders for each type of document
- Keep original documents in a safe place
- Make copies for working files

**Digital Organization:**

- Scan all documents and save in organized folders
- Use consistent file naming conventions
- Back up files to cloud storage
- Keep digital and physical copies synchronized

**Tracking Tools:**

- Create a spreadsheet listing all medical expenses
- Track payments made and outstanding balances
- Monitor insurance claim status
- Note follow-up actions needed

## Step 6: Communicate Effectively with Healthcare Providers

### Building Strong Provider Relationships

Your healthcare providers are potential witnesses in your case. Building positive relationships and maintaining clear communication helps ensure they'll provide strong support for your claim.

**Key Communication Strategies:**

**Be Honest and Consistent:**

- Tell the same story about how your injury occurred
- Report symptoms accurately and completely
- Don't exaggerate, but don't minimize either
- Update providers on changes in your condition

**Ask Questions:**

- Request explanations you can understand
- Ask about your prognosis
- Understand your treatment options
- Inquire about long-term effects

**Document Important Conversations:**

- Take notes during appointments
- Ask for written summaries of important discussions
- Request copies of provider communications

- Follow up on verbal instructions in writing

## What to Tell Your Healthcare Providers

**About Your Legal Case:**

- Inform providers that you're pursuing a legal claim
- Explain that their records may be used as evidence
- Ask if they're willing to provide testimony if needed
- Discuss any concerns they may have about involvement

**About Your Incident:**

- Provide clear, consistent details about how the injury occurred
- Explain the timeline of symptom development
- Describe any immediate treatment you received
- Clarify any confusing aspects of your case

# Step 7: Handle Second Opinions and Independent Medical Examinations

## Seeking Second Opinions

A second opinion can strengthen your case by:

- Confirming your initial diagnosis
- Identifying additional injuries or complications
- Providing alternative treatment options
- Supporting your prognosis and future needs

**When to Seek a Second Opinion:**

- You have complex or severe injuries
- Your recovery isn't progressing as expected
- You're facing major surgery or expensive treatment

- Insurance companies are questioning your diagnosis

### Independent Medical Examinations (IMEs)

Insurance companies may require you to undergo an IME with their chosen doctor. These examinations are designed to challenge your claims, so preparation is crucial.

**IME Preparation Tips:**

- Bring all medical records and documentation
- Arrive on time and dress appropriately
- Be honest but don't volunteer unnecessary information
- Stick to the facts about your injuries and limitations
- Don't discuss legal strategy or settlement expectations
- Take someone with you as a witness if allowed

**After the IME:**

- Request a copy of the report
- Review it carefully with your attorney
- Be prepared to challenge inaccurate or biased findings
- Provide additional evidence if needed to counter negative reports

## Step 8: Plan for Future Medical Needs

### Documenting Long-Term Prognosis

Many personal injury cases involve ongoing medical needs. Proper documentation of future requirements is essential for full compensation.

**Future Medical Needs May Include:**

- Ongoing treatment and therapy
- Future surgeries or procedures
- Long-term medication needs

- Medical equipment and devices
- Home modifications for disabilities
- Vocational rehabilitation

**How to Document Future Needs:**

- Ask providers for written opinions about future treatment
- Obtain life care plans from qualified professionals
- Get cost estimates for recommended future care
- Document how injuries may worsen over time
- Consider the impact of aging on your injuries

## Working with Medical Experts

Complex cases may require medical expert testimony to:

- Explain your injuries to a jury
- Counter insurance company medical opinions
- Establish causation between the incident and your injuries
- Provide opinions about future medical needs

**Types of Medical Experts:**

- Treating physicians
- Independent medical experts
- Vocational rehabilitation specialists
- Life care planners
- Economic experts for future cost calculations

## Red Flags That Could Hurt Your Case

## Medical Documentation Mistakes to Avoid

**Treatment Gaps:**

- Long periods without medical treatment
- Cancelled appointments without rescheduling
- Stopping treatment against medical advice

**Inconsistent Reporting:**

- Changing your story about how the injury occurred
- Reporting different symptoms to different providers
- Minimizing symptoms to some doctors while emphasizing them to others

**Non-Compliance Issues:**

- Not following prescribed treatment plans
- Missing multiple appointments
- Failing to take prescribed medications

**Social Media Problems:**

- Posting photos that contradict your claimed limitations
- Discussing your case or injuries online
- Showing activities inconsistent with your restrictions

## Insurance Company Tactics to Watch For

**Surveillance:**

- Private investigators may follow you
- Social media monitoring
- Video recording of your activities

**Medical Record Requests:**

- Requests for unrelated medical history
- Attempts to access mental health records

- Fishing expeditions for pre-existing conditions

**IME Bias:**

- Doctors who consistently find in favor of insurance companies
- Rushed examinations that minimize findings
- Reports that ignore or downplay objective medical evidence

# Technology Tools for Organization

## Digital Documentation Apps

**Medical Record Apps:**

- MyChart (many healthcare systems)
- Health Tap
- Personal health record apps

**Expense Tracking Apps:**

- Mint
- YNAB (You Need A Budget)
- PocketGuard
- Excel or Google Sheets templates

**Pain and Symptom Tracking:**

- MyRA (for arthritis)
- PainScale
- ArthritisPower
- Symple Symptom Tracker

## Cloud Storage Solutions

**Recommended Platforms:**

- Google Drive
- Dropbox
- iCloud
- OneDrive

**Security Considerations:**

- Use strong, unique passwords
- Enable two-factor authentication
- Regularly update access permissions
- Keep sensitive documents encrypted

# Working with Your Attorney

## How Medical Records Support Your Legal Case

Your attorney will use your medical documentation to:

- Establish the extent and severity of your injuries
- Prove causation between the incident and your condition
- Calculate economic damages
- Negotiate with insurance companies
- Present evidence at trial if necessary

## What Your Attorney Needs from You

**Complete Medical Records:**

- All treatment records from the date of injury forward
- Pre-injury medical records that may be relevant
- Billing statements and insurance communications
- Documentation of future medical needs

**Organized Information:**

- Chronological timeline of treatment
- List of all healthcare providers
- Summary of ongoing symptoms and limitations
- Financial impact documentation

**Honest Communication:**

- Full disclosure of all injuries and symptoms
- Information about pre-existing conditions
- Compliance with treatment recommendations
- Any concerns about your medical care

# Maximizing Your Settlement Value

## Strong Medical Documentation Increases Settlement Value

Insurance companies pay more when faced with:

- Clear medical evidence of serious injuries
- Consistent treatment records showing proper care
- Objective medical findings (imaging, test results)
- Professional medical opinions supporting your claims
- Well-documented ongoing symptoms and limitations

## Building the Strongest Possible Case

**Medical Evidence Checklist:**

- [ ] Immediate medical attention after injury
- [ ] Complete diagnostic workup
- [ ] Consistent treatment compliance

- [ ] Thorough documentation of all symptoms
- [ ] Organized financial records
- [ ] Clear prognosis and future needs assessment
- [ ] Expert medical opinions when needed

**Documentation Quality Factors:**

- [ ] All records are complete and legible
- [ ] Treatment timeline shows consistent care
- [ ] Symptoms are well-documented and explained
- [ ] Financial impact is clearly quantified
- [ ] Future needs are professionally assessed

## Common Medical Documentation Challenges and Solutions

### Challenge: High Medical Costs

**Solutions:**

- Work with providers on payment plans
- Apply for hospital charity care programs
- Use medical credit cards for treatment costs
- Document financial hardship in your case file

### Challenge: Insurance Coverage Issues

**Solutions:**

- Appeal denied claims with medical documentation
- Use your attorney's experience with insurance companies
- Document all interactions with insurers
- Consider using health insurance and seeking reimbursement later

### Challenge: Provider Reluctance to Get Involved

**Solutions:**

- Explain the importance of their cooperation
- Offer to minimize their time commitment
- Use medical record requests instead of live testimony when possible
- Work with providers who understand legal cases

### Challenge: Complex or Multiple Injuries

**Solutions:**

- See appropriate specialists for each injury
- Keep detailed records of how injuries interact
- Use a master timeline to track all treatment
- Consider hiring a case manager for complex medical needs

## Special Considerations for Different Types of Injuries

### Brain Injuries and Concussions

**Special Documentation Needs:**

- Neuropsychological testing
- Cognitive assessment results
- Impact on work and daily functioning
- Family member observations of changes

### Spinal Injuries

**Critical Documentation:**

- MRI and CT scan results
- Orthopedic and neurological evaluations
- Physical therapy progress notes
- Impact on mobility and independence

### Soft Tissue Injuries

**Strengthening Your Case:**

- Consistent treatment records
- Objective findings when possible
- Impact on daily activities documentation
- Long-term prognosis from specialists

### Psychological Injuries

**Important Elements:**

- Professional mental health treatment
- Impact on relationships and work
- Connection to the traumatic incident
- Medication and therapy records

## Final Checklist: Is Your Medical Documentation Complete?

### Immediate Post-Injury (First 30 Days)

- [ ] Sought medical attention within 24 hours
- [ ] Obtained copies of all emergency treatment records
- [ ] Followed up with primary care physician
- [ ] Started personal injury journal

- [ ] Set up medical record filing system

### Ongoing Treatment (Throughout Recovery)

- [ ] Attended all scheduled appointments
- [ ] Followed all treatment recommendations
- [ ] Kept detailed personal injury journal
- [ ] Collected all medical bills and insurance documents
- [ ] Maintained organized filing system

### Case Preparation

- [ ] Obtained complete medical records from all providers
- [ ] Organized all financial documentation
- [ ] Documented future medical needs
- [ ] Prepared medical timeline
- [ ] Reviewed records for accuracy and completeness

### Working with Legal Team

- [ ] Provided complete medical documentation to attorney
- [ ] Discussed medical aspects of case strategy
- [ ] Prepared for potential medical expert testimony
- [ ] Reviewed settlement demands with medical evidence in mind

## Conclusion: Your Medical Records Tell Your Story

Your medical documentation is more than just paperwork - it's the foundation of your personal injury case and the proof of how the incident has impacted your life. By following the comprehensive strategies outlined in this guide, you'll build a strong evidentiary foundation that supports your claim and maximizes your potential recovery.

Remember that thorough medical documentation serves two crucial purposes: ensuring you receive the medical care you need to recover and providing the evidence necessary to secure fair compensation for your injuries. The time and effort you invest in properly documenting your medical treatment will pay dividends throughout your case and recovery process.

**Key Takeaways:**

- Seek immediate medical attention and follow all treatment recommendations
- Keep detailed, organized records of all medical treatment and expenses
- Document the daily impact of your injuries through a personal journal
- Work closely with your healthcare providers and legal team
- Stay organized and proactive throughout the entire process

Your commitment to thorough medical documentation demonstrates to insurance companies, attorneys, and potentially a jury that your injuries are real, serious, and deserving of fair compensation. By following this guide, you're taking an important step toward both your physical recovery and the success of your legal claim.

# 8

# Preserving Evidence and Building a Record

## *Types of Evidence, How to Get and Preserve Them*

When you've been injured due to someone else's negligence, your medical records tell only part of your story. While doctors document your physical injuries and treatment, winning your personal injury case requires a much broader collection of evidence that proves what happened, who was at fault, and how the incident has impacted every aspect of your life.

Think of evidence as the building blocks of your case. Each piece - whether it's a photograph, text message, or witness statement - helps construct a complete picture that supports your right to compensation. Without proper evidence, even the most legitimate claims can fail in court or result in inadequate settlements.

This comprehensive guide will walk you through every type of evidence you should preserve, provide step-by-step instructions for collecting and organizing it, and help you avoid common mistakes that could seriously damage your case.

# Physical and Visual Evidence

## The Power of Seeing is Believing

Visual evidence often has the greatest impact on judges, juries, and insurance adjusters because it provides an immediate, visceral understanding of what happened and the severity of your injuries.

## Critical Photos to Take Immediately

**At the Accident Scene:**

- Multiple angles of vehicle damage, including close-ups and wide shots
- The exact position where vehicles came to rest
- Skid marks, debris, and impact points
- Street signs, traffic signals, and road markings
- Weather conditions and lighting
- Any obstructions to visibility (trees, buildings, parked cars)
- License plates of all vehicles involved

**Your Injuries:**

- Document injuries immediately after the accident, even if they seem minor
- Continue photographing throughout your recovery to show progression
- Include bruising, swelling, cuts, and any visible trauma
- Photograph medical devices (casts, braces, wheelchairs, crutches)
- Show how injuries affect your daily activities

**Property Damage:**

- All damaged personal property (clothing, glasses, electronics, jewelry)

- Interior damage to your vehicle (broken seats, deployed airbags)
- Any safety equipment that was damaged (helmets, protective gear)

## Video Evidence

Modern smartphones make it easy to capture video evidence that can be even more powerful than photographs:

- Record a walkthrough of the accident scene, narrating what you see
- Film the damage to all vehicles from multiple angles
- Document any mechanical issues (strange noises, leaking fluids)
- Record witness statements on the spot (with their permission)
- Film your daily struggles during recovery to show impact on quality of life

## Preserving Physical Items

**What to Keep:**

- Damaged clothing worn during the accident
- Any safety equipment (helmets, protective gear)
- Personal items damaged in the incident
- Product pieces if the case involves defective products
- Any debris from the accident scene

**How to Preserve:**

- Store items in labeled bags or containers
- Avoid cleaning or repairing damaged items
- Take photos before moving or storing anything
- Keep items in a secure, dry location
- Document where and when each item was collected

# Electronic Evidence in the Digital Age

## Text Messages and Digital Communications

Your phone likely contains a wealth of evidence that could support your case. Text messages, emails, and app-based communications can establish timelines, prove fault, and document the impact of your injuries.

**Messages to Preserve:**

- Conversations with anyone involved in the accident
- Communications with employers about missed work
- Messages with family and friends about your condition
- Texts with medical providers or insurance companies
- Social media direct messages related to the incident

**How to Preserve Digital Messages:**

*For Text Messages:*

1. Take screenshots of entire conversations, not just individual messages
2. Ensure timestamps and contact information are visible
3. Save screenshots to cloud storage immediately
4. Consider using your phone's built-in backup features
5. Never delete messages, even if they seem unimportant

*For Email:*

1. Forward important emails to a dedicated folder
2. Export emails as PDF files when possible
3. Include full headers showing sender, recipient, and timestamp
4. Back up entire email accounts during litigation

## Dashcam and Security Camera Footage

Dashboard cameras and security systems often capture the crucial moments before, during, and after an accident, providing objective evidence that can be more reliable than witness testimony.

**Immediate Steps for Dashcam Footage:**

1. Check if any vehicle involved has a dashcam (including commercial vehicles)
2. Ask to review footage immediately at the scene
3. Request copies from other drivers or their insurance companies
4. Back up your own dashcam footage to multiple locations
5. Note the exact time settings on the camera

**Security Camera Sources to Investigate:**

- Traffic cameras at intersections
- Business security systems (stores, restaurants, gas stations)
- Residential doorbell cameras and security systems
- ATM cameras
- Public transportation cameras

**Important:** Many systems automatically delete footage after 24-72 hours. Contact property owners immediately to request preservation of relevant footage.

## Smartphone Data and Location Services

Your smartphone silently collects detailed data that can provide crucial evidence in personal injury cases.

**Valuable Smartphone Data:**

- GPS location history showing where you were when the accident occurred
- Movement and activity data from health apps
- Phone usage logs that might show distracted driving by other parties

- Photos with embedded GPS coordinates and timestamps
- Accelerometer data that might indicate the force of impact

**How to Access and Preserve This Data:**

*For iPhone Users:*

1. Go to Settings > Privacy & Security > Location Services > System Services > Significant Locations
2. Export Health app data: Health app > Profile > Export All Health Data
3. Download your data from iCloud if you use it
4. Screenshot your Screen Time data if relevant

*For Android Users:*

1. Visit Google Takeout (takeout.google.com) to download your data
2. Access Google Timeline for location history
3. Export data from Google Fit or other health apps
4. Review Google Photos for automatically backed-up images

**Working with Forensic Experts:** Your attorney may hire digital forensics experts who can:

- Recover deleted data from devices
- Authenticate digital evidence for court
- Extract metadata from photos and files
- Analyze phone usage patterns
- Create demonstrative exhibits from digital data

## Social Media Evidence Strategy

### The Double-Edged Sword of Social Media

Social media can significantly help or hurt your personal injury case. While insurance companies and defense attorneys will scrutinize your social media presence looking for evidence that contradicts your claims, properly managed social media can actually support your case.

## What Social Media Evidence Can Prove

**Positive Uses:**

- Document your pain and suffering through sincere posts about your condition
- Show limitations in your daily activities
- Preserve encouraging messages from friends and family
- Document missed life events and activities
- Establish your pre-accident lifestyle and activities

**Evidence That Could Hurt Your Case:**

- Photos or videos showing physical activities that contradict claimed limitations
- Posts about travel or activities that suggest you're not as injured as claimed
- Check-ins at locations when you claim to be homebound
- Comments or posts that minimize your injuries
- Evidence of risk-taking behavior or illegal activities

## Best Practices for Social Media During Your Case

**Do:**

- Preserve all existing content with screenshots and archives
- Continue normal, honest posting about your condition and recovery
- Document genuine struggles and limitations you're experiencing
- Save supportive messages from friends and family
- Keep detailed records of what you post and when

**Don't:**

- Delete or edit existing posts (this can be seen as destroying evidence)
- Post photos or videos of physical activities without considering how they might be interpreted
- Accept new friend requests from unknown people (they might be investigators)
- Post about your case details or legal strategy
- Ignore privacy settings - assume everything is public

**Privacy Settings Are Not Absolute Protection:** Even with strict privacy settings, courts can order the production of social media content in litigation. The best approach is to be mindful of everything you post rather than relying solely on privacy controls.

### Archiving Your Social Media Content

**Tools and Methods:**

- Use Facebook's "Download Your Information" feature
- Export Twitter data through their archive tool
- Screenshot Instagram posts and stories
- Save Snapchat content before it disappears
- Use third-party archiving tools with your attorney's guidance

## Building Your Personal Injury Evidence File

### Creating a Centralized Evidence System

Organization is crucial for managing the large volume of evidence in a personal injury case. A well-organized system ensures nothing gets lost and makes it easier for your attorney to build a strong case.

### Essential Components of Your Evidence File

**Physical Evidence Inventory:**

- Photographs (organized by date and subject)

- Videos with descriptions and timestamps
- Physical items with documentation of how they were obtained
- Medical records and bills
- Police reports and incident documentation

**Digital Evidence Archive:**

- Backed-up smartphone data
- Social media archives
- Email communications
- Text message screenshots
- Dashcam or security footage

**Document Organization System:** Create folders (physical and digital) for:

- Medical Documentation
- Insurance Communications
- Employment Records
- Witness Information
- Expert Reports
- Legal Correspondence

## Technology Tools for Organization

**Cloud Storage Solutions:**

- Google Drive, Dropbox, or OneDrive for backup and accessibility
- Ensure strong passwords and two-factor authentication
- Share access with your attorney as needed
- Regularly back up new evidence

**Spreadsheet Tracking:** Create a master spreadsheet with columns for:

- Date

- Type of evidence
- Description
- Source
- Location/storage
- Relevance to case
- Notes

### Working with Your Attorney on Evidence Management

**Regular Communication:**

- Update your attorney immediately when you discover new evidence
- Ask which evidence is most important for your specific case
- Understand how different types of evidence will be used
- Get guidance on evidence you're unsure about preserving

**Professional Evidence Collection:** Your attorney may arrange for:

- Professional accident reconstruction
- Expert analysis of digital evidence
- Formal witness interviews
- Medical expert examinations
- Economic loss calculations

## Your Personal Injury Recovery Journal

### The Power of Documentation

A detailed recovery journal serves multiple purposes in your personal injury case: it helps you remember important details, documents the full impact of your injuries, and prepares you for depositions and trial testimony.

### What to Document Daily

**Physical Condition:**

- Pain levels (use a 1-10 scale consistently)
- Location and type of pain (sharp, dull, throbbing, burning)
- Mobility limitations and improvements
- Sleep quality and disturbances
- Medication taken and side effects
- Physical therapy progress and setbacks

**Emotional and Mental Impact:**

- Mood changes and emotional struggles
- Anxiety or depression related to the accident
- Impact on relationships with family and friends
- Frustration with limitations
- Progress in mental health treatment

**Daily Life Limitations:**

- Activities you couldn't perform or had difficulty with
- Missed work days and reasons
- Social events or family activities you couldn't attend
- Household tasks you couldn't complete
- Hobbies or interests you had to abandon or modify

**Financial Impact:**

- Medical expenses and co-pays
- Lost wages or reduced income
- Transportation costs for medical appointments
- Home modifications or equipment needed
- Additional expenses caused by your injuries

## Journal Writing Tips

**Be Consistent:**

- Write entries at the same time each day
- Don't skip days, even if you feel "normal"
- Use the same format and rating scales
- Date and time each entry

**Be Honest and Detailed:**

- Record both good days and bad days
- Don't exaggerate, but don't minimize either
- Use specific examples rather than general statements
- Include quotes from doctors, therapists, or family members

**Focus on Changes:**

- Compare your current abilities to pre-accident condition
- Note any improvements or setbacks
- Document new symptoms or complications
- Record when you're able to resume activities

## Sample Journal Entry Format

**Date: [Date] Pain Level (1-10): [Number]**

**Physical Condition:**

- Woke up with severe lower back stiffness (8/10 pain)
- Could barely get out of bed without assistance
- Took prescribed pain medication at 7 AM and 3 PM
- Attended physical therapy - completed 20 minutes instead of usual 45 due to pain

- Right leg numbness continued throughout the day

**Activities/Limitations:**

- Unable to drive to appointment - spouse had to take time off work
- Couldn't lift grocery bags
- Had to use shower chair again
- Missed daughter's soccer game due to inability to sit in bleachers

**Emotional Impact:**

- Felt frustrated and guilty about spouse missing work
- Disappointed about missing another family event
- Worried about when I'll be able to return to normal activities

**Medical/Treatment:**

- Dr. Smith recommended continuing current medication
- Physical therapist noted decreased range of motion in left shoulder
- Next MRI scheduled for [date]

# Witness Information and Statements

## The Importance of Witness Testimony

Witnesses provide independent, third-party accounts of what happened and can be crucial in establishing fault and the severity of your injuries. Their testimony can corroborate your version of events and provide details you might have missed due to shock or injury.

## Types of Witnesses to Identify

**Eyewitnesses to the Accident:**

- Other drivers, passengers, or pedestrians who saw what happened
- People in nearby businesses or residences
- Construction workers or road crews in the area

- Public transportation operators or passengers

**Character Witnesses:**

- Family members who can testify about how your injuries have affected your daily life
- Friends who can describe changes in your personality or abilities
- Coworkers who observed your work performance before and after the accident
- Coaches, trainers, or activity partners who can testify about lost abilities

**Expert Witnesses:**

- Medical professionals who treated you
- Accident reconstruction specialists
- Economic experts who can calculate lost wages and future earning capacity
- Life care planners who can project future medical needs

## Collecting Witness Information

**At the Scene:**

- Get names, phone numbers, and addresses of all witnesses
- Ask for their insurance information if they were involved in the accident
- Find out what they saw and heard
- Ask if they would be willing to give a formal statement later
- Take photos of their driver's licenses or business cards

**Follow-Up Contact:**

- Reach out to witnesses within 24-48 hours while memories are fresh
- Ask them to write down what they remember
- Request recorded or written statements

- Get their preferred contact information for future communication
- Ask if they know of any other witnesses

## Obtaining Witness Statements

**Written Statements Should Include:**

- The witness's name and contact information
- Their location at the time of the accident
- A detailed description of what they observed
- Weather and road conditions
- The behavior of all parties involved
- Any statements made by the parties at the scene
- The witness's signature and date

**Recorded Statements:**

- Use your smartphone to record audio or video statements
- Get the witness's permission before recording
- Ask them to state their name and the date at the beginning
- Have them describe what they saw in their own words
- Ask follow-up questions to clarify important details
- Save recordings immediately to cloud storage

## Working with Reluctant Witnesses

Some witnesses may be hesitant to get involved. Here's how to approach them:

**Address Their Concerns:**

- Explain that their testimony could help prevent similar accidents
- Assure them that providing a statement doesn't necessarily mean they'll have to testify in court

- Let them know they can consult with an attorney if they have concerns
- Respect their decision if they ultimately decline to participate

**Make It Convenient:**

- Offer to meet them at their preferred location
- Be flexible with timing
- Provide written questions in advance if they prefer
- Keep initial conversations brief and focused

# Chain of Custody and Evidence Integrity

## Why Evidence Integrity Matters

For evidence to be admissible in court, you must be able to prove that it hasn't been tampered with, altered, or fabricated. This is called maintaining the "chain of custody," and it's crucial for the credibility of your case.

## Documenting How You Obtained Evidence

**For Physical Evidence:**

- Record the date, time, and location where you found or collected each item
- Note who was present when you collected the evidence
- Describe the condition of the item when you found it
- Take photos before moving or storing anything
- Keep detailed notes about where items are stored

**For Digital Evidence:**

- Screenshot or export data immediately after an incident
- Note the source and method of collection
- Record timestamps and metadata when possible

- Use write-protected storage media when appropriate
- Maintain backup copies in multiple locations

## Storage and Handling Best Practices

**Physical Evidence Storage:**

- Use clear, labeled containers or bags
- Store items in a secure, climate-controlled environment
- Avoid handling items unnecessarily
- Don't attempt to clean or repair damaged items
- Document anyone who has access to stored evidence

**Digital Evidence Management:**

- Use read-only access when possible
- Create checksums or hashes to verify file integrity
- Store original files separately from working copies
- Maintain detailed logs of who accessed files and when
- Use professional-grade backup systems

## Working with Forensic Experts

Your attorney may hire forensic experts to:

- Authenticate digital evidence
- Recover deleted data from devices
- Analyze accident scenes using 3D modeling
- Examine vehicles for mechanical defects
- Create demonstrative exhibits for trial

## Common Evidence Preservation Mistakes

## Mistakes That Can Damage Your Case

Even with the best intentions, it's easy to make errors that could compromise your evidence or hurt your case. Here are the most common mistakes and how to avoid them.

## Digital Evidence Mistakes

**Deleting or Altering Content:**

- Never delete text messages, emails, or social media posts
- Don't edit photos or videos, even to improve quality
- Avoid updating or changing privacy settings during litigation
- Don't "clean up" your social media presence

**Failing to Act Quickly:**

- Many digital records are automatically deleted after short periods
- Security camera footage often overwrites itself within days
- Phone data can be lost if devices are damaged or reset
- Online content can be removed by third parties

**Inadequate Backup:**

- Store evidence in multiple locations
- Use cloud storage and physical backups
- Test backup systems regularly
- Don't rely on a single storage method

## Physical Evidence Mistakes

**Contamination or Damage:**

- Handle physical evidence as little as possible
- Don't attempt to clean or repair damaged items
- Store evidence in appropriate containers

- Protect evidence from environmental damage

**Poor Documentation:**

- Always photograph evidence before moving it
- Record detailed notes about how evidence was collected
- Label everything clearly with dates and descriptions
- Maintain detailed inventories

### Communication Mistakes

**Talking Too Much:**

- Be careful what you say to insurance adjusters
- Don't speculate about fault or blame
- Avoid discussing your case on social media
- Be cautious in communications with the other party

**Not Communicating Enough:**

- Keep your attorney informed of new evidence
- Report changes in your condition immediately
- Don't assume evidence is unimportant
- Ask questions if you're unsure about anything

## Working with Your Attorney on Evidence

### The Attorney-Client Partnership

Your relationship with your personal injury attorney is a partnership, and evidence collection is a collaborative effort. Understanding your role and your attorney's role will help ensure nothing important is overlooked.

### What Your Attorney Will Handle

**Professional Evidence Collection:**

- Obtaining official police reports and government records
- Subpoenaing records from hospitals and other medical providers
- Hiring expert witnesses and forensic specialists
- Conducting formal depositions of witnesses
- Requesting production of documents from other parties

**Legal Analysis:**

- Determining which evidence is most important for your case
- Understanding rules of evidence and admissibility
- Developing strategies for presenting evidence effectively
- Identifying weaknesses in the other side's evidence
- Preparing evidence for trial or settlement negotiations

## Your Role in Evidence Collection

**Initial Preservation:**

- Secure evidence immediately after the accident
- Take photographs and collect witness information
- Preserve electronic communications and data
- Begin documenting your injuries and recovery
- Organize and maintain your evidence files

**Ongoing Documentation:**

- Keep detailed records of your recovery progress
- Document new symptoms or complications
- Maintain your injury journal consistently
- Preserve any new communications or evidence
- Report significant developments to your attorney

### Communication with Your Attorney About Evidence

**Regular Updates:**

- Schedule regular check-ins to discuss new evidence
- Report any attempts by insurance companies to obtain evidence
- Inform your attorney of any evidence you discover
- Ask questions about evidence you're unsure about preserving

**Evidence Sharing:**

- Provide your attorney with copies of all evidence
- Use secure methods to share sensitive information
- Organize evidence clearly before sharing
- Maintain your own backup copies

## Special Considerations for Different Types of Cases

### Motor Vehicle Accidents

**Unique Evidence Needs:**

- Vehicle inspection reports and repair estimates
- Traffic camera footage and police reports
- Cell phone records to prove distracted driving
- Black box data from vehicles
- Maintenance records for commercial vehicles

**Timing Considerations:**

- Vehicles may be repaired or destroyed quickly
- Traffic camera footage has short retention periods
- Witnesses may be harder to locate later
- Road conditions can change rapidly

## Slip and Fall Cases

**Critical Evidence:**

- Photos of the hazardous condition from multiple angles
- Surveillance footage from the property
- Maintenance records and inspection reports
- Weather reports and lighting conditions
- Witness statements about how long the condition existed

**Property Owner Information:**

- Identify all parties responsible for the property
- Obtain lease agreements and maintenance contracts
- Request incident reports filed by the property owner
- Document any previous similar incidents

## Medical Malpractice Cases

**Medical Records:**

- Complete medical records from all providers
- Imaging studies and test results
- Pharmacy records and medication lists
- Expert medical opinions and reviews
- Documentation of informed consent

**Timeline Documentation:**

- Detailed chronology of all medical care
- Records of all communications with medical providers
- Documentation of when problems were first noticed
- Comparison of condition before and after treatment

### Product Liability Cases

**Product Evidence:**

- The actual defective product (never discard it)
- Packaging, instructions, and warning labels
- Purchase receipts and warranty information
- Similar products for comparison
- Recall notices or safety warnings

**Manufacturing Information:**

- Product serial numbers and manufacturing dates
- Design specifications and safety testing
- Quality control records
- Distribution and sales records
- Previous complaints or lawsuits

## Digital Age Challenges and Opportunities

### Emerging Technologies and Evidence

As technology continues to evolve, new types of evidence become available, but new challenges also arise in preserving and authenticating digital evidence.

### Internet of Things (IoT) Devices

**Smart Home Devices:**

- Smart doorbells and security cameras
- Home automation systems that track activity
- Health monitoring devices and fitness trackers
- Smart appliances that record usage patterns

**Vehicle Technology:**

- Advanced dashcams with cloud backup
- GPS tracking and telematics systems
- Autonomous vehicle sensor data
- Mobile app data from ride-sharing services

## Artificial Intelligence and Deep Fakes

**Authentication Challenges:**

- Sophisticated photo and video manipulation
- AI-generated content that appears authentic
- Deep fake technology that can create false evidence
- Need for advanced forensic analysis

**Protection Strategies:**

- Use blockchain technology for evidence authentication
- Employ advanced digital forensics experts
- Maintain detailed chains of custody
- Verify evidence through multiple sources

## Privacy and Data Protection

**Legal Considerations:**

- Understanding privacy laws and regulations
- Obtaining proper consent for data collection
- Protecting sensitive personal information
- Complying with data retention requirements

**Practical Steps:**

- Use secure storage and transmission methods

- Limit access to sensitive evidence
- Anonymize data when possible
- Work with attorneys who understand privacy law

# Preparing for Depositions and Trial

## How Your Evidence Will Be Used

All the evidence you've carefully preserved will ultimately be used to support your case during settlement negotiations, depositions, and potentially at trial. Understanding how evidence is presented can help you collect it more effectively.

## Settlement Negotiations

**Evidence Packages:**

- Comprehensive evidence packages to insurance companies
- Visual presentations using photos and videos
- Economic calculations supported by documentation
- Medical summaries with supporting records

**Demonstrative Aids:**

- Day-in-the-life videos showing your limitations
- Before-and-after photo comparisons
- Timeline presentations of your recovery
- Economic loss calculations and projections

## Deposition Preparation

**Using Your Journal:**

- Review your injury journal before depositions
- Use specific examples from your documentation

- Refresh your memory about dates and details
- Prepare for questions about your recovery process

**Evidence Authentication:**

- Be prepared to testify about how you collected evidence
- Understand the chain of custody for important items
- Review photographs and videos before testifying
- Practice explaining technical aspects of digital evidence

## Trial Presentation

**Visual Impact:**

- Large-format prints of key photographs
- Video presentations and animations
- 3D models and reconstructions
- Interactive timelines and demonstrations

**Witness Testimony:**

- Expert witnesses to explain technical evidence
- Character witnesses to describe your life changes
- Medical experts to explain your injuries and prognosis
- Economic experts to calculate your losses

# Conclusion: Your Evidence, Your Future

The evidence you preserve today will determine the strength of your personal injury case tomorrow. In our digital age, the types and amount of available evidence have expanded dramatically, but so have the opportunities to make critical mistakes that could compromise your claim.

Remember these key principles:

**Act Quickly:** Many types of evidence have short preservation periods. Security cameras overwrite footage, smartphones lose data when damaged, and witnesses' memories fade. The sooner you begin preserving evidence, the stronger your case will be.

**Be Thorough:** Cast a wide net when collecting evidence. Items that seem unimportant today might become crucial later. Your attorney can help determine what's relevant, but it's better to preserve too much evidence than too little.

**Stay Organized:** A well-organized evidence file makes your attorney's job easier and ensures nothing gets lost. Use technology tools to help manage the large volume of information in modern personal injury cases.

**Work with Professionals:** While you can and should collect much of the initial evidence yourself, don't hesitate to work with your attorney and expert witnesses to ensure evidence is properly preserved, authenticated, and presented.

**Be Patient and Persistent:** Building a strong evidence file takes time and attention to detail. The effort you put in now will pay dividends when it comes time to negotiate a settlement or present your case at trial.

Your injuries have already cost you enough. Don't let inadequate evidence preparation cost you the compensation you deserve. By following the strategies outlined in this guide, you'll be well-positioned to tell your complete story and achieve the best possible outcome for your case.

Remember, every case is unique, and this guide should supplement, not replace, professional legal advice. Work closely with a qualified personal injury attorney who can provide guidance specific to your situation and jurisdiction.

The path to recovery after a personal injury is challenging enough. With proper evidence preservation, you can focus on healing while building the strongest possible case for your future.

9

# Estimating Your Damages

*Figuring Out What Your Case Is Worth*

## Understanding What You're Entitled To

After suffering an injury due to someone else's negligence, understanding your potential compensation is crucial for making informed decisions about your case. This comprehensive guide breaks down everything you need to know about personal injury damages, from immediate medical bills to long-term impacts on your quality of life.

## The Three Types of Damages Explained

Personal injury compensation falls into three distinct categories, each serving a different purpose in making you whole again.

### Economic Damages: Your Out-of-Pocket Losses

Economic damages represent the measurable financial impact of your injury. These are typically the most straightforward to calculate because they come with concrete documentation.

**Medical Expenses** form the foundation of most economic damage claims. This comprehensive category includes:

- Emergency room visits and ambulance transportation
- Hospital stays, including room charges and facility fees
- Surgical procedures and operating room costs
- Diagnostic tests like X-rays, MRIs, and CT scans
- Prescription medications and medical equipment
- Physical therapy and rehabilitation services
- Specialist consultations and follow-up appointments
- Mental health counseling related to your injury
- Future medical care projected by healthcare providers

**Lost Income** encompasses both immediate and future earning losses:

- Wages missed due to medical appointments and recovery time
- Sick leave and vacation time used for injury-related absences
- Lost overtime opportunities and bonuses
- Reduced earning capacity if you can't return to your previous role
- Loss of self-employment income or business profits
- Diminished career advancement opportunities

**Property Damage** covers physical items damaged in the incident:

- Vehicle repair or replacement costs
- Personal electronics like phones or tablets
- Damaged clothing, jewelry, or accessories
- Specialized equipment for work or hobbies

- Home modifications needed for accessibility

**Additional Out-of-Pocket Expenses** might include:

- Transportation costs for medical visits
- Parking fees at medical facilities
- Over-the-counter medications and supplies
- Home care or housekeeping services
- Childcare expenses during recovery
- Assistive devices like crutches or wheelchairs

## Non-Economic Damages: The Human Cost

Non-economic damages address the intangible but very real ways your injury has affected your life. While harder to quantify, these damages often represent the most significant portion of your compensation.

**Pain and Suffering** encompasses both physical and emotional distress:

- Acute pain from the initial injury
- Ongoing discomfort during recovery
- Chronic pain that may persist long-term
- Sleep disruption and fatigue
- Headaches, nausea, or other secondary symptoms
- The mental anguish of dealing with persistent pain

**Emotional and Psychological Impact** recognizes the mental health consequences:

- Anxiety about your recovery or financial situation
- Depression stemming from lifestyle changes
- Post-traumatic stress disorder (PTSD) from the incident
- Fear of similar situations or activities
- Cognitive difficulties affecting memory or concentration

- Social anxiety or withdrawal from relationships

**Loss of Life's Enjoyment** compensates for activities you can no longer pursue:

- Sports and recreational activities you once loved
- Hobbies that require physical abilities you've lost
- Travel limitations due to your condition
- Reduced participation in family gatherings or social events
- Inability to perform household tasks or yard work
- Loss of independence in daily activities

**Relationship Impact** addresses how your injury affects your closest bonds:

- Strain on your marriage or partnership
- Reduced intimacy with your spouse
- Inability to participate fully in parenting activities
- Social isolation from friends and extended family
- Changes in your role within family dynamics

## Punitive Damages: Holding Wrongdoers Accountable

Punitive damages serve a different purpose entirely - they're designed to punish particularly egregious behavior and deter others from similar conduct. These damages are awarded in addition to compensatory damages but only in specific circumstances.

**When Punitive Damages Apply:**

- Drunk driving incidents
- Intentional acts of violence
- Gross negligence by healthcare providers
- Corporate cover-ups of known dangers
- Reckless behavior showing complete disregard for safety

**State-Specific Considerations:**

In California, punitive damages can be substantial when defendants act with malice, oppression, or fraud. The state has no statutory cap on punitive awards, though courts must ensure they're reasonable in relation to the harm caused.

New York takes a more restrictive approach, requiring clear and convincing evidence of gross negligence or intentional wrongdoing. Punitive damages are less common and typically smaller in New York cases.

## Calculating Your Damages: Methods and Approaches

### Economic Damage Calculation

Calculating economic damages requires meticulous documentation and often professional expertise:

**Immediate Costs:** Total all bills, receipts, and documented expenses related to your injury. Include co-pays, deductibles, and out-of-network charges not covered by insurance.

**Future Expenses:** Work with medical professionals to project ongoing care needs. This might include:

- Life care plans developed by rehabilitation specialists
- Medical cost projections adjusted for inflation
- Equipment replacement schedules for assistive devices
- Home modification costs for accessibility

**Lost Income Analysis:** Document your earning history and work with vocational experts to assess:

- Your pre-injury earning trajectory
- The impact of your injury on career advancement
- Transferable skills that might allow different employment
- The difference between your previous and current earning capacity

## Non-Economic Damage Calculation

Courts and attorneys use several methods to value non-economic damages:

**The Multiplier Method** applies a factor to your economic damages based on injury severity:

- Minor injuries (sprains, minor cuts): 1.5-2x economic damages
- Moderate injuries (broken bones, herniated discs): 2-3x economic damages
- Severe injuries (traumatic brain injury, paralysis): 3-5x economic damages
- Catastrophic injuries (permanent disability): 5x+ economic damages

**Example Calculation:**

- Medical bills: $25,000
- Lost wages: $15,000
- Total economic damages: $40,000
- Severity multiplier for herniated disc: 3
- Non-economic damages estimate: $120,000

**The Per Diem Method** assigns a daily value to your pain and suffering:

- Choose a reasonable daily amount (often based on your daily earnings)
- Multiply by the number of days you've suffered and will continue to suffer
- Adjust for varying levels of pain over time

**Example Calculation:**

- Daily pain value: $200 (based on your $75,000 annual salary)
- Days of significant pain: 365 days
- Per diem calculation: $73,000

## Building Your Documentation Strategy

Strong documentation is essential for maximizing your damage recovery. Create a comprehensive record-keeping system from day one.

### Medical Documentation

Maintain complete medical records including:

- All treatment reports and physician notes
- Diagnostic test results and imaging studies
- Prescription records and pharmacy receipts
- Physical therapy progress notes
- Mental health treatment records
- Medical device or equipment receipts

### Financial Documentation

Preserve all economic impact evidence:

- Pay stubs for lost wage calculations
- Tax returns showing earning history
- Bank statements reflecting financial impact
- Receipts for all injury-related expenses
- Insurance correspondence and claim documents
- Employment records showing missed work time

### Personal Impact Documentation

Create a detailed injury journal recording:

- Daily pain levels on a 1-10 scale
- Activities you can no longer perform
- Sleep disruption and quality issues

- Emotional state and mood changes
- Medication effects and side effects
- Interactions with family and friends

### Photographic Evidence

Document your injury's visual impact:

- Immediate post-injury photographs
- Progress photos showing healing or lack thereof
- Visible scars, bruising, or deformity
- Assistive devices or medical equipment
- Home modifications or accessibility changes
- Activities you can no longer perform

## Working with Professional Experts

Complex injury cases often require expert testimony to fully establish your damages.

### Medical Experts

Healthcare professionals can provide crucial testimony about:

- The extent and permanency of your injuries
- Future treatment needs and associated costs
- Disability ratings and functional limitations
- The relationship between your injury and ongoing symptoms
- Quality of life impacts from a medical perspective

### Vocational Rehabilitation Experts

These specialists assess your work-related limitations:

- Your ability to return to previous employment
- Transferable skills for alternative careers
- Wage loss calculations based on diminished capacity
- Retraining needs and associated costs
- Labor market analysis for your situation

### Economic Experts

Financial specialists can project long-term economic impacts:

- Future wage loss calculations with inflation adjustments
- Present value analysis of lifetime economic losses
- Cost-of-living adjustments for different geographic areas
- Investment and retirement impact analysis
- Comprehensive life care cost projections

### Life Care Planners

These professionals develop comprehensive care plans including:

- Detailed medical treatment projections
- Equipment needs and replacement schedules
- Home modification requirements
- Personal care and assistance needs
- Transportation and accessibility considerations

## Maximizing Your Damage Recovery

### Common Mistakes to Avoid

Many injury victims inadvertently reduce their potential compensation by:

- Failing to seek immediate medical attention

- Not following through with prescribed treatment
- Returning to work too soon or against medical advice
- Failing to document the injury's impact on daily life
- Accepting quick settlement offers without full evaluation
- Not considering future medical needs and complications

### Strategic Considerations

Work with your attorney to develop a comprehensive damage strategy:

- Time your medical evaluations for maximum impact
- Consider the tax implications of different damage awards
- Understand how pre-existing conditions might affect your case
- Evaluate structured settlement options for large awards
- Plan for Medicare liens and insurance subrogation rights

### Negotiation Leverage

Strong damage documentation provides negotiation advantages:

- Insurance adjusters take well-documented claims more seriously
- Comprehensive damages packages often lead to faster settlements
- Clear economic projections establish baseline settlement values
- Emotional impact evidence can significantly increase offers
- Expert testimony threats encourage reasonable settlement discussions

## Understanding Settlement vs. Trial Considerations

The strength of your damage documentation influences whether your case settles or goes to trial.

### Settlement Advantages

Most personal injury cases settle, offering benefits like:

- Faster resolution and payment
- Reduced legal costs and fees
- Guaranteed compensation without trial risks
- Privacy and confidentiality
- Reduced stress and emotional toll

## Moving Forward with Confidence

Understanding personal injury damages empowers you to make informed decisions about your case and your future. By documenting your losses comprehensively, working with qualified professionals, and developing a strategic approach to your claim, you'll be positioned to receive fair compensation that truly reflects the full impact of your injury.

Remember that every personal injury case is unique, and the specific circumstances of your situation will influence both the types and amounts of damages available to you. Working with an experienced personal injury attorney ensures that you don't overlook any potential sources of compensation and that your damage calculation reflects the true cost of your injury on every aspect of your life.

The road to recovery - both physical and financial - begins with understanding what you're entitled to receive. Use this knowledge to advocate effectively for yourself and to build the strongest possible foundation for your personal injury claim.

# 10

# Special Considerations for Motor Vehicle Accidents Claims

## *Tips for Handling Car Crash Claims*

Motor vehicle accidents can turn your life upside down in an instant. Beyond the immediate shock and potential injuries, you're suddenly faced with insurance companies, medical bills, and legal complexities that vary dramatically depending on where your accident occurred. If you've been in a car accident in New York or California, understanding your state's specific laws and procedures isn't just helpful - it's essential for protecting your rights and maximizing your recovery.

This comprehensive guide breaks down everything you need to know about handling motor vehicle accident claims in these two major states, each with fundamentally different approaches to liability and compensation.

# Understanding the Two Systems: Your Rights Depend on Your Location

## New York's No-Fault System: Quick Coverage with Limitations

New York takes a unique approach designed to get accident victims the medical care they need quickly, without lengthy legal battles over who caused the crash. Under the no-fault system, your own insurance company pays for your immediate needs regardless of fault - but there's a catch.

**How New York's No-Fault System Works:**

When you're injured in a car accident in New York, your Personal Injury Protection (PIP) coverage kicks in immediately. This mandatory coverage pays for:

- **Medical expenses** from the accident
- **Lost wages** (typically up to 80% of your average weekly wage, capped at a maximum amount)
- **Essential services** you can no longer perform (like childcare or housekeeping)
- **Transportation costs** to medical appointments

The benefit of this system is speed. You don't need to wait for fault determination or negotiate with the other driver's insurance company to get initial coverage. Your medical bills get paid, and you receive some income replacement while you recover.

**The Serious Injury Threshold:**

However, New York's no-fault system comes with a significant limitation. You cannot sue the at-fault driver for pain and suffering damages unless your injuries meet the state's "serious injury" threshold. This threshold includes:

- **Bone fractures** of any kind
- **Significant disfigurement** that affects your appearance
- **Permanent loss of use** of a body part, organ, function, or system
- **A medically determined impairment** that prevents you from

performing substantially all daily activities for at least 90 days during the 180 days immediately following the accident

If your injuries don't meet this threshold, you're limited to your PIP benefits and cannot pursue additional compensation for pain, suffering, or inconvenience - even if the other driver was completely at fault.

## California's At-Fault System: Full Recovery Rights with Proof Requirements

California operates under the traditional fault-based system, which means the driver who caused the accident is financially responsible for all resulting damages. This system offers more comprehensive recovery options but requires you to prove the other driver's negligence.

**How California's At-Fault System Works:**

In California, if another driver causes your accident, you have the right to seek full compensation for:

- **All medical expenses** (past and future)
- **Lost wages and earning capacity**
- **Property damage** to your vehicle
- **Pain and suffering**
- **Emotional distress**
- **Loss of enjoyment of life**

You can pursue this compensation by filing a claim with the at-fault driver's insurance company or by filing a lawsuit. Unlike New York, there's no threshold requirement - any injury caused by another's negligence can form the basis of a claim.

**The Challenge of Proving Fault:**

The trade-off in California's system is that you must prove the other driver was negligent and that their negligence caused your injuries. This requires evidence such as:

- Police reports
- Witness statements

- Accident reconstruction
- Traffic camera footage
- Expert testimony

Without clear proof of the other driver's fault, you may struggle to recover compensation, even for severe injuries.

## Updated Insurance Requirements: What You Must Carry

Understanding minimum insurance requirements is crucial because these amounts often determine how much compensation is available after an accident.

### New York's 2025 Requirements

Every New York driver must carry:

- **Bodily Injury Liability:** \$25,000 per person / \$50,000 per accident
- **Property Damage Liability:** \$10,000 per accident
- **Personal Injury Protection (PIP):** \$50,000 per person
- **Uninsured Motorist Bodily Injury:** \$25,000 per person / \$50,000 per accident

The PIP coverage is what makes New York's no-fault system work, providing immediate benefits regardless of who caused the accident.

### California's Updated Requirements (Effective January 1, 2025)

California increased its minimum requirements to:

- **Bodily Injury Liability:** \$30,000 per person / \$60,000 per accident (increased from \$15,000/\$30,000)
- **Property Damage Liability:** \$15,000 per accident (increased from \$5,000)

These increases recognize that the previous minimums were inadequate for today's medical costs and vehicle values. However, even these new minimums may not fully cover serious accidents.

## The Critical Importance of UM/UIM Coverage

Uninsured Motorist (UM) and Underinsured Motorist (UIM) coverage protects you when the at-fault driver has no insurance or insufficient coverage to compensate you fully.

### Why This Coverage Matters

Consider this scenario: You're seriously injured in an accident caused by a driver with only California's minimum $30,000 in coverage, but your medical bills alone total $75,000. Without UIM coverage, you'd be personally responsible for the $45,000 difference.

**In New York:** UM coverage is mandatory and must match your liability limits, providing built-in protection.

**In California:** UM/UIM coverage is optional, but insurance companies must offer it. This coverage becomes especially important in:

- Hit-and-run accidents where the at-fault driver is never identified
- Accidents with uninsured drivers (unfortunately common)
- Serious accidents where the at-fault driver's minimum coverage is inadequate

### Filing UM/UIM Claims

UM and UIM claims are filed with your own insurance company, but don't assume this makes the process simple. Your insurer may dispute:

- Whether the other driver was truly at fault
- The extent of your injuries
- The value of your claim

Treat UM/UIM claims with the same seriousness as third-party claims, gathering comprehensive evidence to support your case.

## Critical Deadlines: Don't Let Time Run Out

Missing deadlines can completely destroy your case, regardless of how strong your claim might be.

### New York Deadlines

**Immediate Requirements:**

- **DMV Reporting:** Accidents must be reported within 10 days if there's injury or property damage over $1,000
- **No-Fault Claim Filing:** Must file within 30 days of the accident
- **Medical Bill Submission:** Healthcare providers must submit bills within 45 days of treatment

**Lawsuit Deadlines:**

- **Personal Injury:** 3 years from the date of the accident
- **Property Damage:** 3 years from the date of the accident
- **Wrongful Death:** 2 years from the date of death

### California Deadlines

**Immediate Requirements:**

- **DMV Reporting:** Within 10 days if there's injury, death, or damage over $1,000

**Lawsuit Deadlines:**

- **Personal Injury:** 2 years from the date of injury discovery
- **Property Damage:** 3 years from the date of the accident
- **Wrongful Death:** 2 years from the date of death

## Special Considerations That Can Complicate Your Case

## Comparative Negligence: When You Share Some Fault

Both New York and California follow comparative negligence rules, meaning your compensation is reduced by your percentage of fault. For example, if you were 20% at fault for an accident and your damages total $100,000, you'd recover $80,000.

**Pure Comparative Negligence:** Both states follow "pure" comparative negligence, meaning you can recover damages even if you were 99% at fault (though your recovery would be minimal).

Understanding how fault is determined and disputed becomes crucial for maximizing your recovery.

## Vehicle Defect Cases: When the Car Itself Caused the Accident

Sometimes accidents result from vehicle defects rather than driver error. Common defect-related accidents include:

- Brake failures
- Steering system malfunctions
- Tire blowouts due to manufacturing defects
- Airbag failures that worsen injuries

In these cases, you may have a product liability claim against the vehicle manufacturer in addition to any claims related to driver fault.

## Commercial Vehicle Accidents: Higher Stakes, Different Rules

Accidents involving commercial vehicles like trucks, buses, or rideshare vehicles often involve:

- **Higher insurance coverage** due to commercial policy requirements
- **Multiple potentially liable parties** (driver, trucking company, vehicle owner)
- **Federal regulations** that may have been violated

- **Electronic logging devices** and other evidence sources
- **Specialized legal standards** for commercial drivers

These cases typically require more intensive investigation and legal expertise.

## Your Step-by-Step Action Plan After an Accident

Taking the right steps immediately after an accident can significantly impact your case outcome.

### At the Scene

1. **Ensure Safety First**
    - Call 911 immediately
    - Move to safety if possible
    - Check for injuries and request medical attention
2. **Document Everything**
    - Take photos of all vehicles, damage, the accident scene, road conditions, and traffic signs
    - Get contact and insurance information from all drivers
    - Collect contact information from witnesses
    - Note the exact location, time, and weather conditions
3. **Be Careful What You Say**
    - Don't admit fault or apologize
    - Stick to factual observations when speaking to police
    - Be polite but don't speculate about cause

### After Leaving the Scene

1. **Seek Medical Attention**
    - Get evaluated even if you feel fine - adrenaline can mask injuries

    - Follow all treatment recommendations
    - Keep detailed records of all medical care

2. **Report the Accident**
    - File required DMV reports within deadlines
    - Notify your insurance company promptly
    - In New York, file your no-fault claim within 30 days

3. **Preserve Evidence**
    - Keep all medical records and bills
    - Document lost wages
    - Save receipts for accident-related expenses
    - Keep a pain journal if you're experiencing ongoing symptoms

4. **Consult an Attorney**
    - Especially important if you've suffered serious injuries
    - Essential if fault is disputed
    - Critical if dealing with commercial vehicles or multiple parties
    - Valuable for navigating insurance company tactics

## Working with Insurance Companies: Protect Your Interests

Insurance companies are businesses focused on minimizing payouts. Understanding their tactics helps you protect your interests.

### Common Insurance Company Strategies

- **Quick, Low Settlement Offers:** Often made before you fully understand your injuries
- **Requesting Recorded Statements:** Can be used against you later
- **Disputing Medical Necessity:** Questioning whether treatment was required

- **Surveillance:** Investigating your activities to contradict injury claims
- **Delay Tactics:** Hoping you'll accept less due to financial pressure

### Protecting Yourself

- Don't accept the first settlement offer without understanding your full damages
- Be cautious about recorded statements - consider having an attorney present
- Keep detailed records of all communications with insurers
- Don't sign any releases without legal review
- Understand that insurance adjusters work for the insurance company, not you

## Maximizing Your Recovery: Understanding Damages

The compensation available after a motor vehicle accident extends beyond just medical bills.

### Economic Damages (Calculable Losses)

- **Medical expenses** (past and future)
- **Lost wages** and reduced earning capacity
- **Property damage** (vehicle repair/replacement, personal items)
- **Transportation costs** (rental cars, rideshares to medical appointments)
- **Home modification costs** (if disability requires accessibility changes)

### Non-Economic Damages (Subjective Losses)

- **Pain and suffering** (physical discomfort and limitations)
- **Emotional distress** (anxiety, depression, PTSD)

- **Loss of enjoyment of life** (inability to participate in activities you previously enjoyed)
- **Loss of consortium** (impact on relationship with spouse)

Remember that in New York, non-economic damages are only available if you meet the serious injury threshold.

## When to Hire an Attorney

While not every accident requires legal representation, certain situations make an attorney essential:

### Definitely Hire an Attorney If:

- You've suffered serious injuries requiring extensive treatment
- The other driver's insurance company denies liability
- Multiple parties may be at fault
- The accident involved a commercial vehicle
- You're being offered a settlement that seems inadequate
- The insurance company is requesting extensive documentation or depositions
- Your injuries may have long-term consequences

### How an Attorney Helps

- **Investigating the accident** thoroughly and professionally
- **Dealing with insurance companies** on your behalf
- **Calculating the full value** of your claim, including future damages
- **Negotiating settlements** based on experience with similar cases
- **Representing you in court** if litigation becomes necessary
- **Protecting you from costly mistakes** that could harm your case

## Looking Ahead: What This Means for Your Case

Understanding whether you're dealing with New York's no-fault system or California's at-fault system fundamentally shapes your approach to recovery. In New York, focus on maximizing your PIP benefits while building a case for serious injury if applicable. In California, concentrate on proving the other driver's negligence while documenting all your damages comprehensively.

Regardless of which state you're in, the key to a successful outcome is taking action quickly, preserving evidence, understanding your rights, and getting professional help when the stakes are high. The differences between these systems aren't just legal technicalities - they directly impact your ability to recover the compensation you need to rebuild your life after an accident.

The path forward may seem complex, but with the right knowledge and professional guidance, you can navigate these systems effectively and secure the recovery you deserve. Remember, insurance companies have teams of professionals working to minimize your claim - shouldn't you have someone working just as hard to maximize it?

# 11

# Filing a Claim With Insurance After an Injury

*How to Start Your Insurance Claim the Right Way*

## Understanding Your Rights and Protecting Your Financial Future

Being injured in an accident is overwhelming enough without having to navigate complex insurance processes. Whether you're dealing with a car accident, slip and fall, or workplace injury, understanding how to properly file an insurance claim can mean the difference between receiving fair compensation and being left with mounting medical bills.

This comprehensive guide will walk you through every step of the insurance claims process, help you avoid common mistakes that could cost you thousands, and show you when it's time to get professional help.

## The Two Types of Insurance Claims: What You Need to Know

## First-Party Claims: Using Your Own Insurance

A first-party claim is when you file with your own insurance company. This typically happens in situations like:

**Auto Insurance Examples:**

- Personal Injury Protection (PIP) claims in New York
- Uninsured/Underinsured Motorist (UM/UIM) claims
- Medical payments coverage claims
- Collision or comprehensive claims for vehicle damage

**Other Insurance Examples:**

- Homeowner's insurance for slip and fall injuries on your property
- Workers' compensation claims through your employer's coverage
- Disability insurance claims

**Why File First-Party Claims:**

- Faster processing and payment
- Your insurance company has a contractual duty to you
- No need to prove fault in many cases
- Coverage often includes immediate medical expense payments

## Third-Party Claims: Going After the At-Fault Party's Insurance

A third-party claim is filed against the insurance company of the person or business responsible for your injuries. This is the primary way to seek compensation for:

- Pain and suffering
- Full medical expenses
- Lost wages and future earning capacity
- Property damage beyond your own coverage limits

**Important Reality Check:** Third-party insurers represent their policyholder, not you. Their goal is to pay as little as possible while protecting their insured from liability.

## Essential Documentation: Building Your Strongest Case

The strength of your claim depends heavily on the evidence you provide. Missing or incomplete documentation is one of the top reasons claims are denied or undervalued.

### Immediate Post-Accident Documentation

**At the Scene (If Possible):**

- Take photos from multiple angles showing vehicle positions, damage, road conditions, traffic signs, and any visible injuries
- Record video with narration describing what happened
- Get contact information for all parties involved
- Collect witness names, phone numbers, and brief statements
- Note weather conditions, time of day, and any relevant environmental factors

**Police/Incident Reports:**

- Always request a police report for vehicle accidents
- For other incidents (slip and fall, workplace injury), ensure an incident report is filed
- Get the report number and information on how to obtain copies
- Follow up to ensure the report accurately reflects what happened

### Medical Documentation Strategy

**Immediate Medical Care:**

- Seek medical attention immediately, even if you feel fine

- Be honest and thorough when describing your symptoms
- Follow all treatment recommendations
- Keep detailed records of all appointments, treatments, and medications

**Ongoing Medical Records:**

- Request copies of all medical records, test results, and imaging studies
- Maintain a file with treatment summaries from each provider
- Document how your injuries affect your daily activities
- Keep a pain journal with daily entries about symptoms and limitations

**Medical Bills and Expenses:**

- Save every medical bill, pharmacy receipt, and insurance explanation of benefits
- Track mileage to medical appointments
- Document costs of medical equipment (crutches, braces, etc.)
- Keep receipts for over-the-counter medications and supplies

## Employment and Financial Documentation

**Lost Wages Proof:**

- Obtain a letter from your employer stating your regular wages and time missed
- Collect pay stubs from before and after the accident
- If self-employed, gather tax returns and bank statements showing income loss
- Document any vacation or sick time used for injury-related absences

**Future Earning Capacity:**

- Get documentation of any permanent work restrictions

- Obtain employer statements about promotional opportunities you may have missed
- Consider vocational rehabilitation assessments for severe injuries

## Step-by-Step Claim Filing Process

### Step 1: Immediate Notification

**Timing is Critical:**

- Notify your insurance company within 24 hours if possible
- Report to the at-fault party's insurer within 72 hours
- Some policies require immediate notification or risk coverage denial

**What to Report Initially:**

- Date, time, and location of the incident
- Brief description of what happened (stick to facts)
- Names and contact information for all parties involved
- Police report number if applicable
- Initial description of injuries and property damage

### Step 2: Formal Claim Submission

**Required Forms:**

- Complete all claim forms thoroughly and accurately
- Don't leave blank spaces - write "N/A" if something doesn't apply
- Make copies of everything before submitting
- Submit forms via certified mail or email with read receipts

**Documentation Package:**

- Organized medical records with a cover summary
- Clear, labeled photographs

- Police report and witness statements
- Employment verification and wage loss documentation
- Receipts and bills organized chronologically

### Step 3: Ongoing Communication Strategy

**Written Communication Best Practices:**

- Follow up all phone calls with written summaries sent to the adjuster
- Use email when possible to create automatic documentation
- Keep detailed logs of all communications with dates, times, and participants
- Request written confirmation of any agreements or important information

**Sample Follow-Up Email:** "Dear [Adjuster Name], Thank you for our phone conversation today at [time]. I wanted to confirm our discussion about [specific topics]. As we discussed, I will provide [specific documents] by [date], and you indicated that [adjuster's commitments]. Please let me know if I've misunderstood anything. I look forward to your response."

## Mastering Insurance Adjuster Interactions

### Understanding the Adjuster's Role

Insurance adjusters are trained professionals whose job is to investigate claims and minimize payouts. While many are fair and professional, remember that they work for the insurance company, not for you.

**Red Flags in Adjuster Behavior:**

- Pressuring you to settle quickly
- Requesting extensive unrelated medical records
- Asking leading questions about fault
- Making lowball offers without explanation
- Delaying responses to reasonable requests

## Strategic Communication Guidelines

**Do's:**

- Be polite and professional at all times
- Stick to factual information about the accident and your injuries
- Ask for requests in writing
- Take notes during every conversation
- Ask for the adjuster's name, phone number, and claim number
- Request explanation of any coverage denials in writing

**Don'ts:**

- Don't give recorded statements without legal consultation
- Don't admit fault or speculate about what might have happened
- Don't discuss previous injuries or unrelated medical conditions
- Don't accept the first settlement offer
- Don't sign releases without understanding what you're giving up
- Don't let adjusters pressure you into quick decisions

## Medical Records Requests

**What Adjusters Can Legitimately Request:**

- Records directly related to your current injuries
- Treatment records from the date of accident forward
- Pre-existing conditions that may have been aggravated by the accident

**What You Should Limit or Refuse:**

- Complete lifetime medical history
- Mental health records unrelated to the accident

- Treatment for unrelated conditions
- Family medical history

**How to Respond:** "I'm happy to provide medical records directly related to my accident injuries. Please specify exactly which records you need and the relevant time period."

# Critical Timelines by State

## New York Specific Requirements

**No-Fault Insurance Claims:**

- File no-fault application within 30 days of accident
- Submit medical bills within 45 days of treatment (or risk denial)
- Wage loss claims must be filed within 90 days
- Death benefits claims within 2 years

**Third-Party Claims:**

- No specific notification timeline, but sooner is better
- Personal injury lawsuit must be filed within 3 years
- Government entity claims require notice within 90 days
- Property damage claims must be filed within 3 years

**Special New York Considerations:**

- Serious injury threshold must be met to sue for pain and suffering
- No-fault benefits are primary for economic losses up to policy limits
- Comparative fault rules apply to third-party claims

## California Specific Requirements

**Insurance Claims:**

- No specific notification requirements, but prompt reporting is essential

- Government entity claims require notice within 6 months
- Personal injury lawsuits must be filed within 2 years
- Property damage claims have 3-year statute of limitations

**Unique California Rules:**

- Pure comparative negligence (you can recover even if mostly at fault)
- No no-fault insurance system
- Uninsured motorist coverage mandatory unless specifically rejected
- Proposition 213 limits uninsured drivers' recovery rights

# Avoiding Costly Mistakes

## Documentation Errors

**Missing Deadlines:**

- Set calendar reminders for all important dates
- Submit claims well before deadlines
- Follow up to confirm receipt of all submissions
- Keep proof of timely delivery (certified mail receipts, email confirmations)

**Incomplete Medical Documentation:**

- See a doctor immediately, even if injuries seem minor
- Follow all treatment recommendations
- Don't skip appointments or physical therapy
- Report all symptoms, even if they seem unrelated

## Communication Mistakes

**Saying Too Much:**

- Avoid detailed recorded statements without legal advice

- Don't speculate about fault or what others were thinking
- Stick to simple facts: "The light was green when I entered the intersection"
- Don't discuss settlement expectations early in the process

**Accepting Quick Settlements:**

- Insurance companies often make fast, low offers hoping you'll accept
- You may not know the full extent of your injuries immediately
- Consider future medical costs and long-term impacts
- Get a second opinion on settlement offers over $10,000

### Financial Planning Mistakes

**Not Accounting for Future Costs:**

- Long-term physical therapy or medical treatment
- Future surgeries or procedures
- Permanent disability accommodations
- Lost future earning capacity
- Impact on career advancement

## When Professional Help Becomes Essential

### Clear Indicators You Need an Attorney

**Serious Injury Cases:**

- Injuries requiring surgery or long-term treatment
- Permanent disability or disfigurement
- Traumatic brain injuries or spinal cord damage
- Injuries affecting your ability to work

**Complex Liability Situations:**

- Multiple parties involved in the accident
- Disputes about who was at fault
- Government entities involved
- Commercial vehicles or business premises

**Insurance Company Problems:**

- Claim denial without reasonable explanation
- Unreasonably low settlement offers
- Bad faith tactics or delayed responses
- Requests for excessive documentation

**High-Value Claims:**

- Medical bills exceeding $25,000
- Significant lost wages or earning capacity
- Claims involving pain and suffering
- Wrongful death cases

## What to Expect from Legal Representation

**Initial Consultation:**

- Most personal injury attorneys offer free consultations
- Bring all documentation and correspondence
- Ask about fee structures (most work on contingency)
- Understand what services will be provided

**Attorney Responsibilities:**

- Handle all insurance company communications
- Gather additional evidence and expert witnesses
- Calculate fair settlement values
- Negotiate aggressively on your behalf

- File lawsuits when necessary
- Protect you from insurance company tactics

# Settlement Negotiation Strategies

## Understanding Settlement Value

**Economic Damages (Calculable Losses):**

- Past and future medical expenses
- Lost wages and earning capacity
- Property damage
- Out-of-pocket expenses

**Non-Economic Damages (Subjective Losses):**

- Pain and suffering
- Emotional distress
- Loss of enjoyment of life
- Impact on relationships

## Negotiation Tactics

**Building Your Case:**

- Present well-organized documentation packages
- Include day-in-the-life summaries showing impact
- Obtain expert opinions when helpful
- Document ongoing symptoms and limitations

**Responding to Offers:**

- Don't accept the first offer (it's typically 10-30% of fair value)
- Respond with specific reasons why the offer is inadequate

- Counter with documentation supporting your position
- Be prepared to justify your demands

**Sample Response to Low Offer:** "Thank you for your settlement offer of $X. After reviewing the offer against my documented damages, I believe it significantly undervalues my claim. My medical expenses alone total $Y, and this doesn't account for ongoing treatment needs, lost wages of $Z, or the significant pain and impact on my daily life. I would like to discuss a more appropriate settlement in the range of $A based on the attached documentation."

## Special Situations and Considerations

### Government Entity Claims

**Special Rules Apply:**

- Much shorter notice periods (90 days in NY, 6 months in CA)
- Specific claim forms required
- Different immunity and liability rules
- Often lower settlement amounts due to caps

**Common Government Entity Cases:**

- Accidents on public roads or sidewalks
- Injuries at public buildings or facilities
- School district incidents
- Public transportation accidents

### Commercial and Business Claims

**Additional Complexity:**

- Multiple insurance policies may apply
- Corporate liability investigation needed
- Professional liability considerations

- Higher settlement potential but more resistance

### Uninsured Motorist Situations

**Your Options:**

- File with your own UM/UIM coverage
- Pursue the at-fault driver personally (often not worthwhile)
- Check for other potential insurance coverage (employer, family policies)

## Technology and Modern Claims Processing

### Digital Documentation

**Photo and Video Strategy:**

- Take photos immediately at the scene
- Use video to narrate what happened
- Document property damage from multiple angles
- Show the full scene context, not just damage
- Take follow-up photos of injuries as they develop

**Cloud Storage and Organization:**

- Upload all documents to secure cloud storage
- Organize files by date and category
- Share access with your attorney if you hire one
- Keep backup copies of everything

### Communication Technology

**Email Best Practices:**

- Use email for most adjuster communications

- Request read receipts for important messages
- Create folders to organize claim correspondence
- Print and file important email exchanges

**Mobile Apps and Tools:**

- Use voice recording apps for detailed incident recollections
- Photo apps with date/location stamps
- Expense tracking apps for accident-related costs
- Calendar apps for medical appointments and deadlines

# Financial Recovery and Moving Forward

## Managing Expenses During Claims Process

**Immediate Financial Strategies:**

- Use health insurance for immediate medical care
- Apply for short-term disability if available
- Consider personal loans for essential expenses
- Communicate with creditors about your situation

**Long-Term Financial Planning:**

- Consider how settlement funds should be invested
- Plan for potential tax implications of settlements
- Set aside funds for future medical needs
- Consider structured settlements for large amounts

## Recovery and Rehabilitation Focus

**Maximizing Your Recovery:**

- Follow all medical advice consistently

- Attend physical therapy and rehabilitation
- Document your recovery process
- Stay engaged in treatment even when insurance is delayed

**Quality of Life Considerations:**

- Don't let the claims process consume your life
- Seek emotional support when needed
- Focus on healing while protecting your legal rights
- Consider counseling for trauma or anxiety

## Conclusion: Taking Control of Your Claim

Filing an insurance claim after an injury doesn't have to be overwhelming if you approach it systematically and protect yourself at every step. Remember these key principles:

**Be Proactive:** Document everything, meet all deadlines, and stay engaged in the process.

**Be Strategic:** Understand that insurance companies are businesses focused on minimizing payouts, and adjust your expectations and tactics accordingly.

**Be Patient:** Fair settlements take time, and rushing often leads to accepting less than you deserve.

**Be Informed:** Knowledge is power in insurance negotiations, and understanding the process puts you in control.

**Know When to Get Help:** Complex cases, serious injuries, and resistant insurance companies require professional assistance.

Your injury claim may be one of many for the insurance company, but it's your financial future and well-being at stake. By following the strategies in this guide, staying organized, and protecting your rights throughout the process, you'll maximize your chances of receiving fair compensation and focusing on what matters most: your recovery.

Remember: The insurance claims system can be navigated successfully by informed consumers, but don't hesitate to seek professional help when the stakes are high or the process becomes overwhelming. Your health and financial security are worth protecting with every tool available.

# 12

# No-Fault Insurance in New York

## *What It Means and How It Works for You*

Getting into a car accident is stressful enough without having to worry about who's at fault or how you'll pay for medical bills. New York's no-fault insurance system was created to help accident victims get the care and financial support they need quickly, without waiting for lengthy legal battles to determine blame.

However, this system comes with important rules, deadlines, and limitations that every New York driver should understand. This guide will walk you through everything you need to know about no-fault insurance, from what it covers to when you can step outside the system to pursue additional compensation.

### Understanding No-Fault Insurance: The Basics

#### What Makes New York Different

Unlike many states where you must prove the other driver caused your accident to get compensation, New York operates under a "no-fault" system. This means your own insurance company pays for your basic expenses after an accident, regardless of who was responsible for the crash.

This system, officially called Personal Injury Protection (PIP), is designed with one primary goal: getting you the medical care and financial support you need as quickly as possible, without the delays that come with determining fault or going to court.

### The Philosophy Behind No-Fault

The no-fault system recognizes a simple truth: when you're injured in a car accident, you need medical treatment immediately, not months or years later after a lawsuit concludes. By removing the need to prove fault for basic coverage, the system ensures that:

- Medical bills get paid promptly
- Lost wages are partially replaced quickly
- Essential services are covered while you recover
- The court system isn't overwhelmed with smaller injury claims

## What No-Fault Insurance Covers: Your Benefits Explained

New York's standard no-fault coverage provides four main types of benefits. Understanding each category helps you maximize your coverage and avoid unexpected gaps.

### Medical Expenses: Comprehensive Healthcare Coverage

Your no-fault insurance covers all necessary and reasonable medical treatment related to your accident injuries, including:

**Immediate Care:**

- Emergency room visits and ambulance transportation
- Hospital stays and surgical procedures

- Urgent care and walk-in clinic visits
- Diagnostic tests like X-rays, MRIs, and CT scans

**Ongoing Treatment:**

- Physical therapy and occupational therapy
- Chiropractic care and massage therapy
- Mental health counseling for accident-related trauma
- Prescription medications and medical equipment
- Dental work necessitated by the accident

**Specialized Services:**

- Rehabilitation services and speech therapy
- Home healthcare and nursing services
- Medical transportation for treatment appointments
- Prosthetic devices and mobility aids

**Important Note:** The treatment must be "necessary and reasonable," meaning it should be appropriate for your specific injuries and provided by qualified healthcare professionals. Your insurance company may require pre-authorization for certain expensive procedures or treatments.

## Lost Wages: Protecting Your Income

No-fault insurance recognizes that injuries often prevent you from working, creating financial hardship on top of physical pain. The system provides wage replacement benefits with these parameters:

**Coverage Amount:** Up to 80% of your gross lost earnings, subject to a monthly cap of $2,000 **Duration:** Up to three years from the date of the accident **Documentation Required:**

- Verification from your employer confirming your wages and time missed
- Medical documentation from your treating physician stating you're unable to work

**Examples of How This Works:**

- If you earn $3,000 per month, you'd receive $2,000 (the maximum allowed)
- If you earn $2,000 per month, you'd receive $1,600 (80% of your wages)
- If you earn $1,500 per month, you'd receive $1,200 (80% of your wages)

**Self-Employed Individuals:** You can still claim lost wages, but you'll need to provide additional documentation such as tax returns, profit and loss statements, and detailed records of lost business opportunities.

## Essential Services: Daily Life Support

Accidents don't just affect your ability to work - they can impact your ability to handle basic daily tasks. No-fault insurance provides up to $25 per day for essential services for up to one year, including:

**Transportation Assistance:**

- Rides to medical appointments
- Transportation to physical therapy sessions
- Getting to and from work if you can return to limited duties

**Household Help:**

- Cleaning services when you can't maintain your home
- Grocery shopping and meal preparation assistance
- Childcare help when your injuries prevent normal parenting activities
- Lawn care and basic home maintenance you can't perform

**Other Necessary Services:**

- Pet care if your injuries prevent you from caring for animals
- Assistance with banking and essential errands
- Help with personal care tasks if needed

### Death Benefits: Supporting Families

In the tragic event that someone dies in a covered accident, no-fault insurance provides a $2,000 death benefit to the deceased person's estate. While this amount may seem modest compared to the family's loss, it's designed to help with immediate expenses while the family pursues other forms of compensation.

## Who's Covered Under No-Fault Insurance

Understanding who receives no-fault benefits is crucial, as coverage extends beyond just the vehicle's occupants.

### Covered Individuals

**Vehicle Occupants:**

- The driver of the insured vehicle
- All passengers in the insured vehicle, regardless of their relationship to the policyholder
- Passengers in other vehicles involved in the accident (covered by their vehicle's policy)

**Pedestrians and Cyclists:**

- Pedestrians struck by a covered vehicle
- Bicyclists hit by a covered vehicle
- People using wheelchairs, skateboards, or similar devices

### Important Exclusions

**Motorcyclists:** New York's no-fault system specifically excludes motorcycles and their passengers. Motorcyclists must rely on their own health insurance and pursue compensation through traditional liability claims against at-fault drivers.

**Commercial Vehicles:** Some commercial vehicle situations may have different coverage rules, particularly for vehicles with specialized commercial insurance policies.

# How to File a No-Fault Claim: Step-by-Step Process

Filing a no-fault claim correctly and on time is essential to receiving your benefits. Missing deadlines or failing to provide required documentation can result in claim denial.

## Immediate Steps After an Accident

**At the Scene:**

1. Seek medical attention if injured, even if injuries seem minor
2. Call police to file an accident report
3. Exchange insurance information with other drivers
4. Document the scene with photos if safely possible
5. Get contact information from witnesses

**Within 24-48 Hours:**

1. Contact your insurance company to report the accident
2. Begin keeping detailed records of all expenses and medical appointments
3. Follow up with medical care if symptoms develop or worsen

## The 30-Day Rule: Critical Deadline

You must notify your insurance company of the accident within 30 days. This notification should include:

- Date, time, and location of the accident
- Description of how the accident occurred
- Names and contact information of other parties involved
- Police report number if available
- Initial description of your injuries

**Pro Tip:** Even if your injuries seem minor initially, report the accident immediately. Some injuries don't manifest symptoms for days or weeks after an accident.

## Completing the NF-2 Form

The NF-2 form (Application for No-Fault Benefits) is your formal request for benefits. This comprehensive form requires:

**Personal Information:**

- Your contact details and insurance policy information
- Employment information including salary and job duties
- Details about the accident and your injuries

**Medical Information:**

- Names and addresses of all treating healthcare providers
- Description of injuries and treatments received
- Ongoing medical needs and restrictions

**Financial Information:**

- Documentation of lost wages
- Records of out-of-pocket expenses
- Information about other insurance coverage

## Medical Provider Requirements

Healthcare providers treating accident victims must submit bills within 45 days of providing treatment. As a patient, you should:

- Inform all providers that your treatment is related to a car accident
- Provide your insurance information at each appointment
- Keep copies of all medical records and bills
- Follow up if you notice providers haven't submitted claims

### Supporting Documentation for Lost Wages

To receive wage replacement benefits, you'll need:

**From Your Employer:**

- Letter confirming your employment and salary
- Documentation of time missed from work
- Job description outlining your physical requirements

**From Your Doctor:**

- Medical reports detailing your injuries
- Statements about your work restrictions
- Ongoing assessment of your ability to return to work

## Understanding the Limitations: What No-Fault Doesn't Cover

While no-fault insurance provides valuable immediate coverage, it's important to understand what it doesn't include.

### The $50,000 Coverage Cap

Standard no-fault coverage is limited to $50,000 per person per accident. This might seem like a substantial amount, but it can be exhausted quickly in serious accidents:

**Example Scenario:**

- Emergency room visit and initial treatment: $15,000
- Surgery and hospital stay: $25,000
- Physical therapy over six months: $8,000
- Lost wages for three months: $6,000
- **Total:** $54,000 (exceeding the $50,000 limit)

### No Pain and Suffering Compensation

No-fault insurance only covers economic losses - the actual bills and quantifiable financial impacts of your accident. It doesn't compensate for:

- Physical pain and discomfort
- Emotional distress and anxiety
- Loss of enjoyment of life activities
- Impact on relationships and family life
- Permanent scarring or disfigurement (unless it meets certain thresholds)

## Common Exclusions That Can Deny Coverage

Your no-fault claim may be denied if:

**Driver Behavior Issues:**

- You were driving under the influence of alcohol or drugs
- You were committing a felony at the time of the accident
- You intentionally caused your own injuries

**Vehicle Use Issues:**

- Using the vehicle for commercial purposes without proper coverage
- Racing or engaging in speed contests
- Using an unregistered or uninsured vehicle

**Claim Filing Issues:**

- Missing the 30-day notification deadline
- Failing to submit required forms or documentation
- Providing false or misleading information

## When You Can Sue Outside the No-Fault System

The no-fault system's limitations mean that seriously injured individuals may need additional compensation beyond what PIP provides. New York law allows you to "step outside" the no-fault system and pursue a traditional personal injury lawsuit if your injuries meet specific criteria.

## The "Serious Injury" Threshold

To file a lawsuit for pain and suffering damages, your injury must qualify as "serious" under New York Insurance Law Section 5102(d). The law defines serious injury in several specific categories:

### Category 1: Significant Disfigurement

This covers permanent, visible changes to your appearance that meaningfully impact your life. Examples include:

- Severe facial scarring from broken glass
- Burns that leave permanent marks on visible areas
- Disfigurement that affects your professional or social life
- Scarring that requires ongoing cosmetic treatment

**Legal Standard:** The disfigurement must be more than minor scarring. Courts consider factors like the size, location, and permanence of the disfigurement, as well as its impact on your daily life.

### Category 2: Bone Fractures

Any fracture of a bone qualifies as a serious injury, regardless of the bone's size or the complexity of the break. This includes:

- Simple fractures that heal completely
- Compound fractures requiring surgery
- Stress fractures
- Facial bone fractures
- Rib fractures

**Important Note:** Even if the fracture heals perfectly and causes no long-term problems, it still qualifies as a serious injury for lawsuit purposes.

## Category 3: Permanent Limitation of Use

This category covers situations where you've permanently lost some function of a body part or organ. Examples include:

- Reduced range of motion in a joint that doesn't improve with treatment
- Partial loss of vision or hearing
- Nerve damage causing permanent numbness or weakness
- Organ damage affecting function

**Legal Standard:** The limitation must be permanent, meaning it's not expected to improve significantly with time or treatment.

## Category 4: Significant Limitation of Use

This covers temporary but substantial limitations that significantly impact your ability to perform normal activities. The limitation must be:

- More than minor or mild
- Substantial enough to affect your daily life meaningfully
- Documented by objective medical evidence

**Examples:**

- Inability to lift your arm above shoulder height for several months
- Difficulty walking that persists for an extended period
- Cognitive issues that affect your work performance

## Category 5: The 90/180 Day Rule

If your injury prevents you from performing substantially all of your normal daily activities for at least 90 of the first 180 days after the accident, it qualifies as serious. This category recognizes that some injuries may not be permanent but still have a major impact on your life.

**What Counts as "Normal Daily Activities":**

- Work responsibilities and career activities

- Household tasks and family responsibilities
- Recreational activities and hobbies
- Social interactions and community involvement
- Personal care and self-maintenance

**Documentation Requirements:**

- Detailed medical records showing your limitations
- Evidence of missed work or reduced work capacity
- Documentation of activities you couldn't perform
- Statements from family, friends, or coworkers about your limitations

## Proving Your Serious Injury: Building Your Case

Meeting the serious injury threshold requires more than just having qualifying injuries - you need proper documentation and often expert medical testimony.

### Medical Documentation Essentials

**Immediate Post-Accident Care:**

- Emergency room records detailing your initial injuries
- Diagnostic imaging showing fractures, soft tissue damage, or other injuries
- Initial treatment plans and medical recommendations

**Ongoing Treatment Records:**

- Progress notes from all treating physicians
- Physical therapy evaluations and progress reports
- Specialist consultations and recommendations
- Updated diagnostic tests showing injury progression or lack of improvement

**Objective Medical Evidence:**

- Range of motion measurements
- Strength testing results
- Neurological examination findings
- Functional capacity evaluations

### The Role of Medical Experts

Insurance companies and defense attorneys often challenge serious injury claims, arguing that injuries aren't as severe as claimed or that limitations are exaggerated. Medical experts help establish:

- The extent and permanence of your injuries
- How your injuries affect your daily life and work capacity
- Whether your limitations are consistent with the objective medical findings
- The need for future medical treatment or accommodations

### Common Challenges to Serious Injury Claims

**Pre-Existing Conditions:** Defense attorneys often argue that your limitations existed before the accident. Strong medical documentation showing your pre-accident condition versus post-accident status is crucial.

**Gaps in Treatment:** Long periods without medical treatment can undermine your claim. Insurance companies argue that if you were truly injured, you would seek consistent treatment.

**Return to Normal Activities:** Social media posts or witness testimony showing you participating in activities you claim to be unable to perform can damage your case.

## Coordinating No-Fault Benefits with Other Insurance

Understanding how no-fault insurance works with your other coverage helps maximize your benefits and avoid gaps in protection.

## Health Insurance Coordination

When no-fault benefits are exhausted or don't cover certain treatments:

**Primary vs. Secondary Coverage:**

- No-fault insurance typically pays first for covered treatments
- Health insurance becomes secondary, covering additional costs
- Some health insurance plans may require reimbursement if you later recover money through a lawsuit

**Advantage of Dual Coverage:**

- Access to a broader network of healthcare providers
- Coverage for treatments not deemed "necessary" under no-fault standards
- Continued coverage if no-fault benefits are exhausted

## Disability Insurance Benefits

**Short-Term Disability:**

- May supplement no-fault wage replacement
- Often provides higher benefit amounts than no-fault insurance
- May cover periods before no-fault benefits begin

**Long-Term Disability:**

- Crucial for injuries that prevent work beyond the three-year no-fault limit
- Often requires different documentation and approval processes
- May coordinate with no-fault benefits to prevent overpayment

## Supplemental No-Fault Coverage

**Additional Personal Injury Protection (APIP):**

- Increases coverage limits beyond the standard $50,000

- Extends wage replacement and medical coverage
- Relatively inexpensive way to increase protection

**Optional Basic Economic Loss (OBEL):**

- Provides coverage for situations not covered by standard no-fault
- May include higher wage replacement limits
- Can be particularly valuable for high-income individuals

# Maximizing Your No-Fault Benefits: Practical Tips

## Working Effectively with Healthcare Providers

**Choose Experienced Providers:**

- Select doctors and therapists familiar with no-fault insurance requirements
- Ensure providers understand the importance of detailed documentation
- Ask providers to clearly link treatments to your accident injuries

**Communication Strategies:**

- Always mention that your treatment is accident-related
- Provide insurance information at every appointment
- Ask for copies of all medical records and reports
- Follow up if you notice billing issues or claim denials

## Documenting Your Case

**Keep Detailed Records:**

- Maintain a daily diary of your pain levels and limitations
- Document all expenses related to your accident and injuries
- Save receipts for transportation, medications, and medical equipment

- Track lost wages and work limitations

**Photography Documentation:**

- Take photos of visible injuries as they heal
- Document property damage to your vehicle
- Photograph any mobility aids or medical equipment you need
- Update photos to show permanent scarring or disfigurement

### Dealing with Insurance Company Requests

**Medical Examinations:**

- Your insurance company may request an Independent Medical Examination (IME)
- Attend all scheduled examinations promptly
- Be honest about your limitations without exaggerating
- Follow up with your own doctor after any IME

**Recorded Statements:**

- Be truthful but careful when giving recorded statements
- Consider consulting with an attorney before giving detailed statements
- Stick to the facts and avoid speculation about fault or future recovery

## Common Mistakes That Can Jeopardize Your Benefits

### Timing and Deadline Errors

**Missing the 30-Day Notification:**

- This is the most common and costly mistake
- Even if you feel fine initially, report the accident immediately

- Late reporting can result in complete benefit denial

**Delayed Medical Treatment:**

- Waiting too long to seek treatment can undermine your claim
- Insurance companies argue that delayed treatment indicates minor injuries
- See a doctor within days of your accident, even for seemingly minor injuries

## Documentation Failures

**Incomplete Medical Records:**

- Failing to inform providers about the accident connection
- Not following through with recommended treatments
- Missing follow-up appointments without valid reasons

**Poor Record Keeping:**

- Losing important documents and receipts
- Failing to document the impact of injuries on daily life
- Not maintaining consistent communication with insurance companies

## Social Media and Public Activity Mistakes

**Contradictory Online Presence:**

- Posting photos or updates that contradict your claimed limitations
- Participating in activities that seem inconsistent with your injuries
- Allowing others to tag you in photos showing activities you claim to be unable to perform

**Public Statements:**

- Discussing fault or blame at the accident scene
- Making statements to other insurance companies without

understanding the implications

- Admitting to activities that might jeopardize your claim

# When to Consider Legal Representation

## Situations That Warrant Attorney Consultation

**Serious Injury Claims:**

- If your injuries meet the serious injury threshold
- When dealing with permanent disabilities or disfigurement
- If you're considering a lawsuit for pain and suffering damages

**Complex Coverage Issues:**

- Multiple insurance policies or coverage disputes
- Coordination problems between different types of insurance
- Denials of legitimate claims

**Significant Financial Impact:**

- High medical bills that approach or exceed coverage limits
- Long-term disability affecting your career
- Need for ongoing medical treatment or care

## How Attorneys Can Help

**Claim Management:**

- Ensuring all deadlines are met and forms are properly completed
- Communicating with insurance companies on your behalf
- Maximizing available benefits under all applicable policies

**Medical Documentation:**

- Working with healthcare providers to ensure proper documentation

- Arranging for expert medical evaluations when needed
- Building a strong foundation for serious injury claims

**Legal Strategy:**

- Evaluating whether your case meets the serious injury threshold
- Pursuing additional compensation through liability claims
- Coordinating no-fault benefits with lawsuit strategies

# Planning for Your Recovery: Long-Term Considerations

## Understanding Your Ongoing Needs

**Medical Treatment:**

- Recognize that some injuries require long-term care
- Plan for the possibility of needing treatment beyond no-fault coverage limits
- Consider how your injuries might affect you years from now

**Career Impact:**

- Evaluate whether your injuries affect your ability to perform your job
- Consider retraining or career changes if necessary
- Understand disability benefits that might be available long-term

**Financial Planning:**

- Budget for ongoing medical expenses not covered by insurance
- Plan for potential reductions in earning capacity
- Consider the long-term financial impact of your injuries

## Building a Support Network

**Healthcare Team:**

- Develop relationships with providers who understand your ongoing needs
- Consider specialists for long-term injury management
- Maintain regular follow-up care even after acute treatment ends

**Professional Support:**

- Consider working with a financial planner if your injuries have long-term earning impact
- Explore vocational rehabilitation services if career changes are necessary
- Connect with support groups for people with similar injuries

## Conclusion: Navigating Your Path Forward

New York's no-fault insurance system provides crucial immediate support after a car accident, but understanding its complexities is essential to maximizing your benefits and making informed decisions about your recovery.

The key takeaways for every New York driver include:

**Act Quickly:** Report accidents immediately and seek medical attention promptly, even for seemingly minor injuries. Missing deadlines can cost you thousands of dollars in benefits.

**Document Everything:** Keep detailed records of your injuries, treatments, expenses, and how the accident affects your daily life. This documentation is crucial whether you're seeking no-fault benefits or considering a lawsuit.

**Understand Your Options:** Know that no-fault insurance is just one piece of your recovery puzzle. If your injuries are serious, you may have additional legal options that can provide more comprehensive compensation.

**Get Professional Help When Needed:** Complex injuries, significant financial impact, or disputes with insurance companies warrant professional legal consultation. An experienced attorney can help navigate the system and protect your rights.

**Plan for the Long Term:** Consider how your injuries might affect you months or years from now, and plan accordingly for ongoing medical needs and potential career impacts.

Remember, the goal of New York's no-fault system is to help you get back to your normal life as quickly as possible. By understanding how the system works and taking the right steps early in the process, you can ensure you receive all the benefits you're entitled to while keeping your options open for additional compensation if your injuries warrant it.

The road to recovery after a car accident can be long and challenging, but understanding your rights and benefits under New York's no-fault insurance system puts you in the best position to focus on healing while protecting your financial future.

# 13

# Insurance Adjuster Tactics

*Don't Get Tricked - Know What to Watch For*

## What You Need to Know Before Your First Call

After filing a personal injury claim, you'll likely receive a call from an insurance adjuster within days. This person may sound friendly, concerned about your wellbeing, and eager to help resolve your claim quickly. However, it's essential to understand their true role: **insurance adjusters work exclusively for the insurance company, not for you.**

Their primary job is to investigate your claim and protect their company's financial interests. This often means finding ways to minimize how much they pay out on your claim. While not all adjusters use underhanded tactics, many are trained in strategies designed to reduce settlements or deny claims altogether.

## The Insurance Industry's "Three D" Playbook

Many insurance companies follow what industry insiders call the "Three D" strategy:

**Delay:** Drawing out the claims process for months or even years, hoping you'll become frustrated, desperate for money, or simply give up. They know that people facing medical bills and lost wages are under financial pressure.

**Deny:** Refusing to accept responsibility for the accident or claiming their policy doesn't cover your specific situation. Sometimes these denials are legitimate, but often they're based on technicalities or questionable interpretations of the policy.

**Defend:** If you don't accept their denial or low offer, they'll aggressively fight your claim, especially if you decide to file a lawsuit. This can involve hiring expensive legal teams and expert witnesses to contest every aspect of your case.

## Red Flag Tactics: What to Watch Out For

### 1. The "Friendly Helper" Approach

**What they do:** The adjuster calls expressing genuine concern for your health and wellbeing. They might say things like, "I want to get this resolved quickly so you can focus on healing" or "Let's work together to settle this fairly."

**Why it's problematic:** This friendly demeanor is designed to build trust and encourage you to share information freely or accept quick settlements.

**Your response:** Be polite but remember their true allegiance. Don't let a friendly tone make you drop your guard.

### 2. Pressure for Quick Settlement

**What they do:** Within days or weeks of your accident, they offer what seems like a reasonable settlement, often accompanied by statements like, "This is a one-time offer" or "We need to close this file quickly."

**Why it's problematic:** At this early stage, you likely don't know the full extent of your injuries, future medical needs, or how the accident will impact your life long-term. Many injuries, especially soft tissue damage, don't fully manifest immediately.

**Your response:** Never accept the first offer. Tell them you need time to fully understand your injuries and damages. A legitimate settlement offer will remain available after you've completed medical treatment.

## 3. Requesting Recorded Statements

**What they do:** Ask you to provide a detailed, recorded account of how the accident happened, often within days of the incident when you're still in pain, on medication, or emotionally traumatized.

**Why it's problematic:** These recordings are scrutinized for any inconsistencies with other statements you've made. Even innocent mistakes or confusion can be used against you later. They're also looking for admissions of fault or statements that minimize your injuries.

**Your response:** In most states, you are **not legally required** to give a recorded statement to the other party's insurance company. Politely decline and say you'll provide written information after consulting with an attorney.

**Script to use:** "I'm still recovering and not ready to give a detailed statement right now. I'll be happy to provide written information once I've had time to process what happened."

## 4. Invasive Medical Record Requests

**What they do:** Present you with broad medical authorization forms that give them access to your entire medical history, including records unrelated to your current injury.

**Why it's problematic:** They're fishing for pre-existing conditions or other health issues they can blame for your current symptoms. They might also look for mental health records or other private information to use against you.

**Your response:** Only authorize release of medical records directly related to your injury. If you've hired an attorney, let them handle all medical record requests.

**What to say:** "I'll only authorize records related to this specific injury. Please provide a limited authorization form that specifies which records you need."

## 5. Minimizing Your Injuries

**What they do:** Suggest that your injuries aren't as serious as you claim, that they were pre-existing, or that they couldn't have been caused by this particular accident.

**Common phrases to watch for:**

- "That seems like a lot of treatment for such a minor accident"
- "Most people recover from these injuries in a few weeks"
- "Are you sure you weren't having back problems before the accident?"

**Your response:** Stick to the facts. Don't downplay your pain or symptoms to seem tough. Follow all medical advice and document everything your doctors tell you.

## 6. Digital Detective Work

**What they do:** Hire private investigators to follow you or extensively monitor your social media accounts, looking for photos or posts that seem inconsistent with your injury claims.

**Real examples:**

- A person claiming back injury posting photos from a friend's wedding where they appear to be dancing
- Someone with a shoulder injury posting about playing catch with their kids
- Check-ins at gyms, sporting events, or vacation destinations

**Your response:**

- Review your privacy settings on all social media platforms
- Avoid posting photos or updates about physical activities
- Be cautious about what others post and tag you in
- Consider taking a break from social media during your claim process

## 7. Shifting Blame to You

**What they do:** In states where fault is shared (comparative negligence), they'll argue that you were partially or completely responsible for the accident to reduce their payout.

**Common blame-shifting tactics:**

- "You were speeding" (even if you were going the speed limit)
- "You weren't paying attention"
- "Your vehicle maintenance caused the accident"
- "You were distracted by your phone"

**Your response:** Preserve all evidence immediately:

- Take photos of the accident scene, vehicle damage, road conditions, and traffic signs
- Get contact information from witnesses
- Obtain a copy of the police report
- Keep records of weather conditions
- Save any dashcam or security camera footage

## How to Protect Yourself: Best Practices

### Communication Guidelines

**Always communicate in writing when possible.** If you must speak by phone, follow up with an email summarizing what was discussed.

**Sample follow-up email:** "Hi [Adjuster Name], Thank you for our phone conversation today. To confirm, we discussed [brief summary]. As I mentioned, I am still receiving medical treatment and am not ready to discuss settlement at this time. I will contact you when I'm ready to move forward. Please direct all future communications to my attorney [if applicable] at [contact information]."

### Document Everything

Create a file (physical or digital) containing:

- All correspondence with the insurance company
- Medical records and bills
- Photos of injuries and property damage

- Witness contact information
- Police reports
- Work absence documentation
- A daily journal of how your injuries affect your life

## Know When to Stop Talking

**Red flag situations where you should end the conversation:**

- The adjuster becomes argumentative or pushy
- They ask you to speculate about things you don't know
- You feel confused, overwhelmed, or pressured
- They ask about your financial situation or urgency to settle

**What to say:** "I need to take some time to think about this. I'll get back to you." Then consult with an attorney.

## Understanding Settlement Pressure

**Why adjusters want quick settlements:**

- Lower payouts before you understand full damages
- Avoid attorney involvement
- Clear cases from their workload
- Meet company quotas and targets

**Your timeline should be based on:**

- Completing all necessary medical treatment
- Understanding long-term effects of your injuries
- Calculating all damages (medical bills, lost wages, pain and suffering)
- Consulting with professionals (doctors, attorneys, financial advisors)

# When to Hire an Attorney

Consider legal representation if:

**The adjuster:**

- Denies your claim without clear justification
- Offers an obviously inadequate settlement
- Uses aggressive or deceptive tactics
- Requests excessive documentation or invasive authorizations
- Suggests you don't need an attorney

**Your situation involves:**

- Serious injuries requiring ongoing treatment
- Permanent disability or disfigurement
- Disputed fault or complex liability questions
- Multiple parties or insurance companies
- Commercial vehicles or business properties

**Benefits of legal representation:**

- Adjusters typically take claims more seriously when an attorney is involved
- Attorneys understand the true value of different types of damages
- Legal professionals can identify bad faith insurance practices
- You'll have someone to handle communications and paperwork
- Attorneys work on contingency, so you don't pay unless you win

## What Changes When You Have an Attorney

Once you hire an attorney, the dynamic shifts significantly:

**Communication:** All contact goes through your lawyer, eliminating pressure tactics and protecting you from saying something harmful to your case.

**Evaluation:** Attorneys have experience valuing claims and can identify damages you might not have considered, such as future medical expenses or loss of earning capacity.

**Negotiation:** Lawyers understand negotiation strategies and won't be impressed by insurance company tactics.

**Litigation threat:** Insurance companies know that attorneys are prepared to file lawsuits if necessary, which often leads to more reasonable settlement offers.

## Red Flags: When Insurance Companies Cross the Line

Some adjuster behaviors may constitute bad faith insurance practices:

**Outright deceptive practices:**

- Misrepresenting policy terms or coverage
- Making settlement offers contingent on not consulting an attorney
- Threatening to withdraw offers if you don't accept immediately
- Refusing to investigate your claim properly

**Unreasonable delays:**

- Taking months to respond to communications
- Repeatedly requesting the same documentation
- Scheduling and canceling appointments without explanation
- Failing to make decisions on clear-cut claims

**If you suspect bad faith:**

- Document all interactions
- Consult with an attorney immediately
- Consider filing a complaint with your state's insurance commissioner
- Know that bad faith practices can result in additional damages beyond your original claim

## Your Rights as a Consumer

**You have the right to:**

- Reasonable time to evaluate settlement offers
- Access to your claim file
- Fair investigation of your claim
- Prompt payment of valid claims
- Legal representation at any point in the process
- File complaints with state insurance regulators

**You are not required to:**

- Accept the first settlement offer
- Give recorded statements to the other party's insurer
- Sign broad medical authorizations
- Meet unreasonable deadlines
- Negotiate without legal help

## Moving Forward: Taking Control of Your Claim

Remember that this is **your** claim, and you have more control than adjusters want you to believe. The insurance company needs to resolve your claim eventually, and they know that treating you unfairly could result in a lawsuit where they might end up paying significantly more.

**Key mindset shifts:**

- You're not asking for a favor; you're seeking compensation you're entitled to
- The adjuster's job is to minimize payouts, not to be fair to you
- Quick settlements usually benefit the insurance company, not you
- Professional legal help is often worth the cost, especially for serious injuries

**Action steps:**

1. Focus on your medical recovery first
2. Document everything related to your claim
3. Don't rush into settlement discussions
4. Consult with an attorney if the claim is complex or valuable
5. Know your rights and don't be intimidated

## Conclusion

Dealing with insurance adjusters doesn't have to be adversarial, but it should always be approached with caution and preparation. By understanding their tactics and knowing how to respond, you can protect your rights and work toward a fair resolution of your claim.

Remember: the insurance company has trained professionals working to minimize your settlement. You deserve to have experienced advocates working just as hard to maximize your compensation. When in doubt, consult with a personal injury attorney who can evaluate your case and advise you on the best path forward.

The goal isn't to be confrontational with adjusters, but to be informed, prepared, and strategic in your interactions. With the right approach, you can navigate the claims process successfully and obtain the compensation you deserve for your injuries and losses.

# 14

# Writing a Powerful Demand Letter

## *Telling Your Story to Get the Best Settlement*

A demand letter is your first formal step toward getting fair compensation after an injury. It's a detailed document that tells the insurance company exactly what happened, how you were hurt, and how much money you deserve. Think of it as your opening argument in settlement negotiations - and often, it's the most important document in your entire case.

### Why Your Demand Letter Matters

Your demand letter serves four critical purposes:

1. **Formal notification.** It officially tells the insurance company you're seeking compensation and starts the settlement clock ticking.

2. **Case summary.** It provides a complete, factual account of your accident and injuries in one organized document.

3. **Evidence presentation.** It showcases all the proof supporting your

claim, from medical records to witness statements.

4. **Settlement proposal.** It establishes your compensation expectations and opens negotiations.

The timing matters too. You'll typically send your demand letter after you've finished medical treatment or your condition has stabilized. This ensures you can accurately calculate all your damages and present a complete picture of your injuries.

## Building Your Demand Letter: Section by Section

### Opening and Introduction

Start with the basics. Identify yourself, state the accident date, and clearly announce your intention to pursue a personal injury claim against the insured party. This should be straightforward and professional - no drama, just facts.

### Statement of Facts

This is where you tell your story. Describe exactly how the accident happened, but stick to objective facts. Include details from police reports, witness accounts, and any official documentation. Avoid emotional language or speculation about what the other party was thinking. Just present what happened, when, and where.

### Establishing Liability

Here's where you make your case for why the other party is legally responsible. Reference specific traffic laws they violated, safety regulations they ignored, or company policies they failed to follow. If there was a traffic citation issued, mention it. If surveillance footage captured the incident, reference it. This section builds the foundation for your entire claim.

### Injuries and Medical Treatment

Provide a comprehensive overview of your injuries and all treatment received. Include immediate emergency care, ongoing treatment, specialists you've seen, procedures you've undergone, and any lasting effects or limitations. Don't minimize your injuries - if you're still experiencing pain or restrictions, say so clearly.

## Economic Damages (Your Financial Losses)

List every dollar you've spent or lost because of this accident:

- All medical expenses (emergency room, doctors, specialists, physical therapy, medications, medical equipment)
- Lost wages (include documentation from your employer)
- Transportation costs for medical appointments
- Home care or assistance expenses
- Any other out-of-pocket costs related to your injury

Attach documentation for everything - receipts, invoices, pay stubs, and employer statements.

## Non-Economic Damages (Pain and Suffering)

This section addresses your intangible losses - the pain, emotional distress, anxiety, depression, and loss of life's enjoyment you've experienced. Reference your personal journal entries documenting daily struggles, statements from family members about changes they've observed, or notes from mental health professionals if applicable.

Don't be shy about describing how the accident has affected your daily life, relationships, hobbies, and overall well-being. These damages are real and compensable.

## Your Compensation Demand

State your total settlement amount clearly and confidently. Explain that this figure reflects both your economic losses and non-economic damages. Make it clear you're open to good-faith negotiations, but don't apologize for seeking fair compensation.

## Professional Closing

Express willingness to resolve the matter amicably while setting a reasonable deadline for response (typically 30 days). Include your contact information and sign the letter.

## Getting the Tone Right

Your demand letter should sound professional, confident, and factual - never emotional, threatening, or desperate. Use clear, concise language and organize information logically with headings and bullet points where appropriate. The goal is making it easy for the insurance adjuster to understand your position and recognize your claim's legitimacy.

## Essential Supporting Documentation

Attach copies (never originals) of all relevant evidence, organized in the same order you reference them in your letter:

- Police or incident reports
- All medical records and bills
- Photos of your injuries, vehicles, and accident scene
- Witness statements and contact information
- Employment records and wage loss documentation
- Correspondence with the insurance company
- Your personal injury journal or diary entries

Label each attachment clearly (Exhibit A, Exhibit B, etc.) and create a comprehensive evidence package.

## Sample Demand Letter Template

[Your Name]

[Your Address]

[City, State, ZIP Code]

[Phone Number]

[Email Address]

[Date]

[Claims Adjuster Name]

[Insurance Company Name]

[Company Address]

[City, State, ZIP Code]

RE: Personal Injury Claim – [Your Name] vs. [Insured's Name]

Claim Number: [Insert if known]

Date of Loss: [Insert Accident Date]

Dear [Adjuster's Name],

I am writing to formally present my demand for settlement in connection with injuries I sustained in a motor vehicle accident that occurred on [Date] at [Location]. This accident was caused by your insured, [Name of Insured], who was clearly at fault for [specific description of negligent behavior].

**STATEMENT OF FACTS**

On [Date], at approximately [Time], I was [describe what you were doing] when your insured [describe their negligent action that caused the accident]. The collision occurred at [specific location with cross streets].

[Provide detailed, factual account of the accident sequence]

Police Officer [Name] responded to the scene and filed Report Number [Number]. The report indicates [relevant findings that support liability].

**LIABILITY**

Your insured is legally responsible for this accident because [specific reasons with legal basis]. [Reference specific traffic violations, safety regulations, or evidence of negligence]. The police report, witness statements, and physical evidence all support this conclusion.

**INJURIES AND MEDICAL TREATMENT**

As a direct result of this collision, I sustained the following injuries:

- [List each injury specifically]
- [Include both immediate and developing symptoms]

My medical treatment included:

- Emergency room treatment at [Hospital] on [Date]
- Treatment with [Primary Care Doctor] from [Date] to [Date]
- [Physical therapy, specialist consultations, diagnostic tests, etc.]
- [Ongoing treatment or limitations]

Despite extensive treatment, I continue to experience [ongoing symptoms, limitations, or restrictions].

**ECONOMIC DAMAGES**

I have incurred the following documented expenses as a direct result of this accident:

Medical Expenses:

- Emergency room: $[Amount]
- Primary care physician: $[Amount]
- Specialists: $[Amount]
- Physical therapy: $[Amount]
- Diagnostic imaging: $[Amount]
- Medications: $[Amount]
- Medical equipment: $[Amount]

Total Medical: $[Total]

Lost Wages:

- Time off work: [Number] days at $[daily rate] = $[Amount]Reduced earning capacity: $[Amount]

Total Lost Income: $[Total]

Other Expenses:

- Transportation to medical appointments: $[Amount]
- Home care assistance: $[Amount]
- [Other relevant expenses]: $[Amount]

Total Other: $[Total]

TOTAL ECONOMIC DAMAGES: $[Total]

**NON-ECONOMIC DAMAGES**

Beyond my financial losses, this accident has caused significant pain, suffering, and disruption to my life. I have experienced:

- Constant pain and discomfort for [duration]
- Sleep disruption and fatigue
- Anxiety and emotional distress
- Inability to participate in [specific activities, hobbies, family events]
- Strain on family relationships
- [Other specific impacts on quality of life]

These impacts are documented in my personal recovery journal and supported by statements from family members and healthcare providers.

**SETTLEMENT DEMAND**

Based on the clear liability of your insured and the extent of my damages, I am demanding settlement in the amount of $[Total Amount] to resolve this claim in full. This figure reflects both my economic losses of $[Amount] and reasonable compensation for my pain, suffering, and life disruption.

I believe this demand is fair and supported by the evidence. I am prepared to discuss this matter in good faith and hope we can reach a mutually acceptable resolution.

Please respond to this demand within 30 days. If we cannot reach a fair settlement, I am prepared to pursue all available legal remedies.

I look forward to your prompt response.

Sincerely,

[Your Signature]

[Your Printed Name]

Attachments:

- Exhibit A: Police Report
- Exhibit B: Medical Records and Bills
- Exhibit C: Photographs
- Exhibit D: Witness Statements
- Exhibit E: Employment and Wage Documentation
- [Continue listing all attachments]

## Pro Tips for Success

**Proofread everything.** Spelling and grammar errors undermine your credibility. Have someone else review your letter before sending.

**Use certified mail.** Send your demand letter via certified mail, return receipt requested, so you have proof of delivery.

**Keep detailed records.** Maintain copies of everything you send and receive. Document all phone calls and communications.

**Be patient but persistent.** Insurance companies often take time to respond. Follow up professionally if you don't hear back within your stated deadline.

**Prepare for negotiation.** Your initial demand is rarely accepted as-is. Be ready to provide additional documentation or justification for your damages.

**Know when to get help.** If your injuries are severe, liability is disputed, or the insurance company is being unreasonable, consider consulting with a personal injury attorney.

## What Happens Next

After sending your demand letter, expect one of several responses:

- **Acceptance:** Rare, but sometimes insurers accept reasonable demands quickly
- **Counteroffer:** More common - they'll propose a lower amount
- **Request for more information:** They may ask for additional documentation
- **Denial:** They may dispute liability or the extent of your damages

Each response requires a different strategy, but your well-crafted demand letter has started the negotiation process and established your position.

## Common Mistakes to Avoid

**Don't exaggerate or lie.** Stick to facts and be honest about your injuries and their impact.

**Don't accept the first offer.** Initial offers are typically low and leave room for negotiation.

**Don't sign anything without understanding it.** Release forms and settlement agreements have legal consequences.

**Don't miss deadlines.** Pay attention to statute of limitations and other time limits.

**Don't handle complex cases alone.** Serious injuries, disputed liability, or uncooperative insurers may require legal representation.

Your demand letter is a powerful tool for getting fair compensation after an injury. By presenting your case clearly, professionally, and with strong supporting evidence, you give yourself the best chance of achieving a satisfactory settlement without going to court. Take your time, be thorough, and don't be afraid to advocate for yourself - you deserve fair compensation for your injuries and losses.

15

# When to Hire a Personal Injury Attorney

## *How to Know When You Need a Lawyer*

After suffering an injury due to someone else's negligence, you face a critical decision: should you handle the insurance claim yourself or hire a personal injury attorney? This choice can significantly impact both your financial recovery and peace of mind during an already stressful time.

The answer isn't always straightforward. While some minor injury cases can be resolved independently, many situations benefit tremendously from professional legal representation. Understanding when to seek help - and what that help entails - can make the difference between a fair settlement and leaving money on the table.

### When You Can Handle a Claim Yourself

In certain limited circumstances, you may successfully navigate a personal injury claim without legal representation. These situations typically involve:

**Minor injuries that heal completely** within a few days or weeks, requiring minimal medical treatment. Think of cases like minor cuts, bruises, or brief muscle strains that don't require ongoing care or result in lasting effects.

**Crystal-clear liability** where fault is undisputed and well-documented. For example, if you're rear-ended while stopped at a red light and the other driver admits fault, liability is rarely contested.

**Minimal financial impact** with low medical bills, no lost wages, and no ongoing treatment needs. When your total damages are under a few thousand dollars, the economics of hiring an attorney may not make sense.

## When You Need Professional Legal Help

The vast majority of personal injury cases benefit from attorney representation, particularly when any of these factors are present:

### Serious or Long-Term Injuries

If your injuries required surgery, extensive medical treatment, physical therapy, or have resulted in permanent impairment or scarring, you need professional help. These cases involve complex medical issues that require expert analysis and substantial financial projections. An attorney understands how to work with medical professionals to document the full extent of your injuries and their impact on your life.

Serious injuries also mean higher stakes. Insurance companies deploy their most experienced adjusters and legal teams when significant money is involved. You need equally skilled representation to level the playing field.

### Disputed Liability

When the other party claims you were partially or entirely at fault for the accident, legal expertise becomes essential. Insurance companies often dispute liability to reduce their payout, even when their insured was clearly responsible. An attorney knows how to investigate accidents, gather evidence, interview witnesses, and work with accident reconstruction experts to establish fault.

In states that follow comparative negligence rules, even partial fault on your part can reduce your compensation. An experienced attorney can minimize claims against you and maximize the other party's responsibility.

## Uncooperative Insurance Companies

Insurance companies are businesses focused on profit, not your wellbeing. When they deny your claim outright, offer unreasonably low settlements, or drag out negotiations hoping you'll accept less, an attorney can intervene effectively. Attorneys understand insurance company tactics and know how to apply pressure through legal channels.

Having legal representation also changes the dynamic entirely. Insurance companies know that attorneys won't hesitate to file lawsuits when necessary, making them more likely to negotiate in good faith.

## Multiple Liable Parties

Accidents involving several potentially responsible parties - such as multi-vehicle crashes, construction site incidents, or accidents on commercial property - require careful legal coordination. Determining which parties bear responsibility and in what proportion requires investigation and legal analysis beyond most people's capabilities.

Multiple parties also mean multiple insurance companies, each trying to minimize their client's responsibility. Coordinating between various insurers while protecting your interests requires professional skill and experience.

## Government Entity Claims

If your injury involves a government agency - whether a city bus accident, dangerous road conditions, or negligent maintenance of public property - special rules apply. Government claims often have much shorter deadlines than private claims, sometimes as brief as 30 to 90 days. The procedures for filing these claims are also more complex and technical.

Missing a government claim deadline or failing to follow proper procedures can permanently bar your claim, regardless of how strong your case might be.

## Future Damages and Long-Term Impact

Perhaps most importantly, if your injuries will require ongoing medical care, have affected your ability to work, or will cause ongoing pain and limitations, you need help calculating and arguing for future damages. This is one of the most complex aspects of personal injury law and where insurance companies most aggressively fight claims.

Future medical expenses, lost earning capacity, and ongoing pain and suffering can represent the largest portion of your claim's value. Without proper legal representation, these damages are often undervalued or overlooked entirely.

## What Personal Injury Attorneys Actually Do

Hiring a personal injury attorney means gaining an advocate who handles every aspect of your case while you focus on recovery. Their services extend far beyond giving legal advice:

**Thorough Investigation**: Attorneys investigate accidents completely, gathering police reports, interviewing witnesses, photographing scenes, and working with experts when necessary. They know what evidence is crucial and how to preserve it before it disappears.

**Comprehensive Damage Evaluation**: Beyond your current medical bills and lost wages, attorneys work with medical professionals, economists, and vocational experts to project future costs and impacts. This ensures nothing is overlooked in calculating your claim's true value.

**Professional Communication**: All interactions with insurance companies, opposing counsel, and other parties go through your attorney. This prevents you from inadvertently making statements that could harm your case and ensures all communications are strategic and purposeful.

**Skilled Negotiation**: Attorneys understand the negotiation process and know how to present your case persuasively. They recognize fair settlement offers versus lowball attempts and know when to push for more or when to recommend accepting an offer.

**Litigation Management**: If settlement negotiations fail, your attorney handles filing lawsuits, managing discovery, taking depositions, and preparing for trial. Most cases settle before trial, but having an attorney willing and able to try your case gives you significant negotiating leverage.

**Avoiding Critical Mistakes**: Perhaps most valuably, attorneys help you avoid common pitfalls that can damage or destroy your case. These include missing important deadlines, giving recorded statements to opposing insurers, signing releases prematurely, or accepting settlements that don't account for future needs.

## Understanding Attorney Fees and Costs

The financial aspect of hiring an attorney concerns many injury victims, but personal injury law operates on a unique fee structure that makes representation accessible even when you can't afford upfront costs.

### Contingency Fee Arrangements

Most personal injury attorneys work exclusively on contingency fees, meaning you pay nothing unless they recover money for you. The standard contingency fee ranges from 33% to 40% of your total recovery, depending on case complexity and whether the case settles or goes to trial.

This arrangement aligns your attorney's interests with yours - they only succeed financially when you do. It also means attorneys are selective about the cases they accept, generally only taking cases they believe have strong chances of success.

### Case Costs and Expenses

Beyond attorney fees, personal injury cases involve various costs and expenses:

- Court filing fees and service costs
- Medical record retrieval and copying fees
- Expert witness fees for accident reconstruction, medical opinions, or economic analysis
- Deposition costs and court reporter fees
- Investigation expenses and photograph costs

Most attorneys advance these costs during your case and recover them from your settlement or award. However, ask specifically whether you're responsible for costs if your case is unsuccessful - policies vary between firms.

### Free Initial Consultations

Nearly all personal injury attorneys offer free initial consultations, typically lasting 30 to 60 minutes. During this meeting, the attorney will review your case details, explain your legal rights and options, and advise whether you need representation.

This consultation is also your opportunity to evaluate the attorney. Come prepared with questions and pay attention to how they communicate, their experience with similar cases, and whether you feel comfortable working with them.

## Making the Most of Your Consultation

To maximize the value of your initial consultation, prepare thoroughly and ask the right questions:

### Essential Questions to Ask

**Experience and Track Record**: Ask specifically about their experience with cases similar to yours. How many cases like yours have they handled? What were the outcomes? While past results don't guarantee future success, experience with similar cases is valuable.

**Personal Attention**: Will the attorney you're meeting with personally handle your case, or will it be passed to junior attorneys or paralegals? Understanding who will actually work on your case helps set proper expectations.

**Communication Style**: How often will they update you on case progress? Do they prefer phone calls, emails, or in-person meetings? What's their typical response time for questions? Clear communication expectations prevent frustration later.

**Fee Structure Details**: Beyond the basic contingency percentage, understand exactly what costs you might be responsible for and under what circumstances. Get fee agreements in writing before proceeding.

**Case Strategy and Timeline**: Ask for their preliminary assessment of your case's strengths and weaknesses, potential timeline, and likely challenges. While these may change as the case develops, initial impressions can be valuable.

### What to Bring

Come prepared with relevant documents and information:

- Police reports and incident documentation
- Medical records and bills related to your injury
- Photographs of the accident scene, your injuries, or property damage
- Insurance correspondence and policy information
- Documentation of lost wages or other financial impacts
- Contact information for witnesses

The more information you can provide, the better the attorney can assess your case and provide meaningful advice.

## The Value Proposition: Why Professional Help Often Pays Off

While hiring an attorney means sharing a portion of your recovery, studies consistently show that injury victims who hire attorneys typically recover significantly more money than those who handle claims independently - even after paying attorney fees.

This happens for several reasons. Attorneys understand the true value of injury claims and don't settle for initial offers that are typically far below fair value. They know how to document and present cases persuasively, and they have the resources to investigate thoroughly and hire experts when necessary.

Perhaps most importantly, attorneys provide leverage. Insurance companies know that attorneys will file lawsuits when necessary and are prepared to take cases to trial. This knowledge makes insurers more willing to offer fair settlements rather than risk larger jury verdicts.

## Moving Forward with Confidence

The decision to hire a personal injury attorney shouldn't be made lightly, but in most cases involving anything beyond truly minor injuries, professional representation provides significant value. The combination of legal expertise, negotiation skills, and resources that attorneys bring to your case typically results in better outcomes than attempting to navigate the process alone.

Remember that initial consultations are free, so there's no financial risk in speaking with an attorney to understand your options. Even if you ultimately decide to handle your case independently, the consultation can provide valuable insights into the process and potential pitfalls to avoid.

Your focus should be on recovery and getting your life back to normal. Letting a qualified professional handle the legal complexities allows you to concentrate on what matters most - your health and wellbeing - while ensuring your legal rights are fully protected and pursued.

# 16

# How to Choose the Right Personal Injury Attorney

## *Finding the Best Lawyer for Your Case*

The attorney you select will shape every aspect of your personal injury case, from initial negotiations with insurance companies to potential courtroom proceedings. Making the right choice means the difference between receiving full compensation for your injuries and settling for far less than you deserve. Beyond financial outcomes, the right attorney transforms what could be an overwhelming legal maze into a manageable process where you feel supported and informed every step of the way.

When you're dealing with medical bills, lost wages, and physical recovery, the last thing you need is additional stress from poor legal representation. A skilled personal injury attorney handles the complex legal work while you focus on healing, but only if you choose wisely from the start.

### Understanding the Stakes of Your Decision

Personal injury cases often involve substantial sums of money and life-changing circumstances. Insurance companies employ teams of experienced lawyers whose primary goal is minimizing payouts. Without equally skilled representation on your side, you're at a significant disadvantage in negotiations. The attorney you choose becomes your advocate, negotiator, and guide through a legal system designed to be challenging for individuals to navigate alone.

Your attorney's experience directly correlates with their ability to accurately value your claim, anticipate insurance company tactics, and present compelling arguments for maximum compensation. This expertise becomes particularly crucial in cases involving long-term disabilities, complex medical issues, or disputed liability where the stakes are highest.

## Beginning Your Search: Research Strategies That Work

Start your attorney search by focusing exclusively on personal injury specialists rather than general practitioners. Personal injury law involves nuanced regulations, evolving case precedents, and specialized negotiation techniques that generalist attorneys may not fully understand. Specialists stay current with changing laws, maintain relationships with medical experts, and understand how to present injury cases most effectively.

**State Bar Directories Provide Essential Information**

Both New York and California maintain comprehensive attorney databases that serve as your starting point for verification and basic information gathering.

For New York cases, the New York State Unified Court System offers detailed attorney profiles including education, admission dates, and any disciplinary actions. California residents can access similar information through the California State Bar Attorney Search, which provides licensing status, practice areas, and professional standing details.

These official sources give you verified information that marketing materials might obscure or omit. Use them to confirm basic qualifications before investing time in further research.

**Legal Referral Services Connect You With Pre-Screened Attorneys**

Local bar associations operate referral services that match clients with attorneys based on case type and geographic location. These services typically pre-screen participating lawyers for licensing, insurance, and ethical standing, providing an additional layer of quality assurance.

Bar association referrals often include attorneys who've committed to offering initial consultations at reduced rates, making it more affordable to interview multiple candidates. Contact your county bar association to learn about available referral programs and their specific screening criteria.

### Online Platforms Offer Client Perspectives

Digital review platforms like Avvo, Martindale-Hubbell, and Google Reviews provide insights into client experiences and peer evaluations. While these platforms require careful interpretation, they offer valuable perspectives on attorney responsiveness, communication style, and case outcomes.

Look for patterns in reviews rather than focusing on individual comments. Multiple mentions of poor communication, missed deadlines, or unsatisfactory outcomes should raise concerns, while consistent praise for specific strengths indicates reliable qualities.

### Personal Recommendations Carry Significant Weight

Recommendations from friends, family members, or colleagues who've experienced personal injury cases provide firsthand insights into attorney performance. These referrals often include details about communication style, fee transparency, and overall satisfaction that you won't find in professional directories.

When receiving personal recommendations, ask specific questions about the case type, outcome, and what made the experience positive or negative. This information helps you evaluate whether the attorney might be a good fit for your specific situation.

## Essential Qualities in Your Personal Injury Attorney

### Specific Experience With Your Case Type

Personal injury law encompasses numerous specialties, from motor vehicle accidents to medical malpractice to workplace injuries. Each area involves distinct legal principles, evidence requirements, and negotiation strategies. An attorney who primarily handles car accident cases may lack the specialized knowledge needed for a complex medical malpractice claim.

Ask potential attorneys about their experience with cases similar to yours, including recent outcomes and unique challenges they've encountered. Request specific examples of how they've handled complications that commonly arise in your type of case.

**Proven Track Record in Settlements and Trials**

Effective personal injury representation requires both strong negotiation skills and trial readiness. Insurance companies often settle cases more favorably when they know the attorney is prepared and capable of taking the case to court if necessary.

During consultations, ask about the attorney's settlement success rate and trial experience. While most personal injury cases settle out of court, your attorney should have actual trial experience and a willingness to litigate when settlement offers are inadequate.

**Clean Professional Standing**

Verify each potential attorney's licensing status and disciplinary history through official state bar websites. Look for any formal complaints, sanctions, or license suspensions that might indicate ethical problems or professional incompetence.

In New York, use the Attorney Online Services portal to check licensing and disciplinary status. California residents can access this information through the State Bar of California Attorney Search function. Clean professional records don't guarantee excellence, but disciplinary issues should definitely influence your decision.

**Clear Communication and Accessibility**

Your attorney should explain legal concepts in terms you understand, respond promptly to communications, and keep you informed about case developments. During initial consultations, pay attention to how well the attorney listens to your concerns and whether their explanations make sense to you.

Ask about their preferred communication methods, typical response times, and how they handle client questions between meetings. Establish clear expectations about communication frequency and methods before signing any agreements.

**Transparent Fee Structure**

Most personal injury attorneys work on contingency fee arrangements, meaning they receive payment only if you win your case. However, fee structures can vary significantly in terms of percentages charged, cost handling, and expense allocation.

Request written information about fee percentages, how costs and expenses are handled, what happens if you don't win, and whether fees change if the case goes to trial. Understand exactly what you'll owe under different scenarios before making your decision.

## Warning Signs That Should Concern You

### Unrealistic Promises About Outcomes

Legitimate attorneys cannot and will not guarantee specific financial results. Personal injury cases involve too many variables, from jury decisions to insurance policy limits, for anyone to promise exact outcomes. Attorneys who make such guarantees are either inexperienced or deliberately misleading you.

Be particularly wary of attorneys who quote specific dollar amounts during initial consultations before thoroughly reviewing your case details and medical records.

### Poor Communication Patterns

If an attorney is difficult to reach during the consultation process, this pattern will likely continue throughout your case. Unreturned phone calls, delayed responses to emails, or failure to explain legal concepts clearly indicate potential problems with case management and client service.

Your case deserves prompt attention and clear communication from the beginning of the attorney-client relationship through final resolution.

### Concerning Professional History

Multiple disciplinary actions, client complaints, or ethical violations suggest patterns of problematic behavior that could affect your case. While single isolated incidents might not disqualify an attorney, repeated issues indicate systemic problems.

Research any disciplinary history thoroughly and ask direct questions about how past issues have been resolved and what changes have been implemented to prevent recurrence.

### High-Pressure Sales Tactics

Reputable attorneys give you time to make informed decisions about representation. Pressure to sign contracts immediately, refusal to provide references, or unwillingness to explain their legal strategy suggests they're more focused on securing clients than providing quality representation.

Take time to compare multiple attorneys and don't let anyone rush you into decisions about something as important as legal representation.

## Making the Most of Attorney Consultations

Schedule consultations with at least two or three attorneys to compare their approaches, experience levels, and communication styles. Most personal injury attorneys offer free initial consultations, making it cost-effective to interview multiple candidates.

### Essential Documents to Bring

Prepare for consultations by gathering relevant documentation that helps attorneys assess your case strength and complexity. Bring copies of accident or police reports, medical records and bills, insurance correspondence, photographs of injuries or property damage, and any witness statements or contact information.

Organized documentation demonstrates your commitment to the case and provides attorneys with the information they need to give you meaningful assessments during the consultation.

### Key Questions to Ask

Use consultation time efficiently by preparing specific questions about the attorney's experience, approach, and expectations for your case. Ask about their experience with similar cases, typical timeline for resolution, potential challenges they foresee, communication preferences, and fee structure details.

Don't hesitate to ask for references from past clients or examples of successful outcomes in cases similar to yours. Professional attorneys should be willing to provide this information or explain why they cannot.

### Evaluating Attorney Responses

Pay attention not just to what attorneys tell you, but how they communicate their knowledge and approach. Look for attorneys who ask thoughtful questions about your case, explain legal concepts clearly, provide realistic timelines and expectations, and demonstrate genuine interest in your situation.

Be cautious of attorneys who seem to rush through consultations, provide vague answers to specific questions, or focus more on their own accomplishments than on understanding your needs.

## Making Your Final Decision

After completing consultations, compare each attorney across the criteria that matter most for your specific situation. Consider their relevant experience, communication style, fee structure, availability, and your overall comfort level with their approach.

Remember that the cheapest option isn't necessarily the best value, especially when significant compensation is at stake. Focus on finding an attorney who offers the right combination of experience, accessibility, and professional competence for your particular case.

Trust your instincts about which attorney you feel most comfortable working with, as personal injury cases often take months or years to resolve. You'll be working closely with your chosen attorney throughout this period, so compatibility and trust are essential elements of a successful attorney-client relationship.

The attorney you select today will influence not just the financial outcome of your case, but your entire experience navigating the legal system during a challenging time in your life. Take the time necessary to make an informed choice that serves your long-term interests and provides the advocacy you deserve.

## Preparing for the Next Phase

Once you've selected your attorney, the focus shifts to building and presenting your case effectively. Understanding the litigation process helps you prepare for what lies ahead and participate more effectively in your own representation.

In our next discussion, we'll walk through each stage of personal injury litigation, from initial case filing through potential trial proceedings. You'll learn what to expect at each phase, how to contribute to your case's success, and what decisions you'll need to make along the way. This knowledge empowers you to be an active participant in your case rather than a passive observer, ultimately contributing to better outcomes and reduced stress throughout the legal process.

17

# Understanding the Lawsuit Process

*What Happens ff Your Case Goes to Court*

## When Negotiation Isn't Enough: Understanding Your Legal Options

Not every personal injury case can be resolved through friendly conversation or insurance negotiations. Sometimes, despite your best efforts and those of your attorney, the other side simply won't offer fair compensation for your injuries. When this happens, filing a lawsuit may be your best - or only - path to justice.

Filing a lawsuit doesn't mean you're giving up on settlement. In fact, many cases that begin with formal litigation still end in negotiated agreements before ever reaching a courtroom. However, initiating the legal process sends a clear message that you're serious about your claim and creates leverage that often leads to better settlement offers.

Think of a lawsuit as opening a door - once you've filed, you have multiple paths available. You can continue negotiating while the case moves forward, participate in formal mediation, or take your case all the way to trial if necessary. The key is that you're no longer at the mercy of the insurance company's timeline or their willingness to engage in good faith discussions.

## The Six Stages of Personal Injury Litigation

### Stage 1: Filing Your Complaint - Getting Your Day in Court

The litigation process officially begins when your attorney files a document called a "complaint" with the appropriate court. This isn't just paperwork - it's your formal accusation against the person or entity that caused your injuries.

Your complaint tells your story in legal terms. It explains what happened to you, why the defendant is responsible, and what compensation you're seeking. This document becomes the foundation of your entire case, so your attorney will craft it carefully to include every important detail while meeting strict legal requirements.

Once your complaint is filed, the defendant has a limited time to respond with their own document called an "answer." In their answer, they'll either admit or deny each of your allegations. They might also raise defenses (reasons why they believe they shouldn't be held responsible) or even file counterclaims against you.

**Critical Timing: The Statute of Limitations**

Perhaps the most important deadline in personal injury law is the statute of limitations - the time limit for filing your lawsuit. Miss this deadline, and your case is over before it begins.

- **New York**: You typically have three years from the date of your injury to file
- **California**: You typically have two years from the date of your injury to file

These deadlines are generally strict, with very few exceptions. Even if you have a strong case, waiting too long can permanently destroy your right to compensation. This is why it's crucial to consult with an attorney as soon as possible after your injury, even if you think you might be able to settle without litigation.

## Stage 2: Discovery - Uncovering the Truth

Discovery is where both sides roll up their sleeves and dig deep into the facts of your case. Think of it as a formal fact-finding mission where each side has the right to demand information from the other. The goal is to ensure that both parties go into trial with a complete understanding of the evidence, preventing surprise attacks and promoting fair resolution.

**The Four Main Discovery Tools:**

**Interrogatories** are written questions that must be answered under oath. These might include questions about your medical history, how the accident happened, or the extent of your injuries. While they may seem straightforward, interrogatories require careful thought - your answers can be used against you later if they're inconsistent with other evidence.

**Requests for Production** are formal demands for documents, photographs, medical records, or physical evidence. In a car accident case, this might include repair estimates, police reports, phone records, or surveillance footage. In a slip-and-fall case, it could include maintenance records, incident reports, or security camera footage.

**Depositions** are perhaps the most important discovery tool. These are sworn, out-of-court interviews conducted in a lawyer's office with a court reporter present. You'll likely be deposed by the defendant's attorney, and your attorney will depose key witnesses from the other side. Depositions can last several hours and cover every aspect of your case in detail.

**Independent Medical Examinations** occur when the defendant's insurance company wants their own doctor to evaluate your injuries. While called "independent," these doctors are hired by the other side and may be looking for reasons to minimize your injuries. Your attorney will prepare you for what to expect and may arrange for you to be accompanied by a medical professional.

## Stage 3: Pre-Trial Motions - Shaping the Legal Battlefield

Before your case reaches trial, both sides may file various motions - formal requests asking the judge to make specific decisions about your case. These motions can significantly impact the outcome of your lawsuit.

A **Motion to Dismiss** argues that even if everything in your complaint is true, you still don't have a valid legal claim. For example, if you were injured while committing a crime, the defendant might argue that you can't recover damages due to your illegal conduct.

A **Motion for Summary Judgment** asks the judge to decide the case without a trial because the important facts aren't in dispute. If successful, this motion can end your case entirely - either in your favor or against you - without ever reaching a jury.

**Motions in Limine** are requests to exclude certain evidence from trial. For instance, if you have a prior criminal conviction unrelated to your accident, your attorney might file a motion to prevent the other side from mentioning it to the jury, arguing that it would be prejudicial and irrelevant.

## Stage 4: Settlement Negotiations and Mediation - Finding Common Ground

Even after litigation begins, settlement remains possible - and likely. In fact, studies show that over 90% of personal injury cases settle before trial. The discovery process often provides both sides with enough information to realistically evaluate the case's strengths and weaknesses.

**Informal settlement talks** can happen at any time. Your attorney and the defendant's attorney might exchange offers and counteroffers through phone calls, emails, or letters. Sometimes a face-to-face meeting can break through impasses that seemed insurmountable in writing.

**Mediation** involves bringing in a neutral third party - usually an experienced attorney or retired judge - to help facilitate settlement discussions. The mediator doesn't make decisions but helps both sides communicate more effectively and explore creative solutions. Mediation is confidential, meaning that nothing said during the process can be used against you if the case goes to trial.

Many courts in New York and California now require parties to attempt mediation before allowing a case to proceed to trial. Even when not required, mediation can be an excellent way to resolve disputes more quickly and cost-effectively than trial.

## Stage 5: Trial - Your Day in Court

If settlement proves impossible, your case will proceed to trial. You'll typically have the choice between a bench trial (decided by a judge) or a jury trial (decided by a panel of your peers). Most personal injury cases are tried before juries, as they tend to be more sympathetic to injured individuals than judges who see these cases regularly.

**The Trial Process:**

**Jury Selection** involves questioning potential jurors to identify those who can fairly decide your case. Both attorneys can exclude jurors who demonstrate bias or prejudice that might affect their judgment.

**Opening Statements** give each side the opportunity to preview their case for the jury. These aren't evidence but rather roadmaps explaining what each side intends to prove and why the jury should rule in their favor.

**Presentation of Evidence** is where your case is won or lost. Your attorney will call witnesses, introduce documents and photographs, and present expert testimony to prove that the defendant caused your injuries and that you deserve compensation.

**Cross-Examination** allows each side to question the other's witnesses. This is where inconsistencies are exposed and credibility is challenged. Skilled cross-examination can sometimes completely undermine an opponent's case.

**Closing Arguments** are each attorney's final opportunity to persuade the jury. They'll summarize the evidence, explain why it supports their client's position, and ask for a specific verdict.

**Jury Instructions and Deliberation** occur after closing arguments. The judge explains the relevant law to the jury, who then retires to deliberate in private. Depending on the complexity of your case, deliberations might last hours or days.

**The Verdict** is the jury's final decision. In personal injury cases, they'll determine whether the defendant is liable and, if so, how much compensation you should receive.

Trials can last anywhere from a few days to several weeks, depending on the complexity of your case and the number of witnesses involved.

## Stage 6: Appeals - When Someone Disagrees with the Outcome

Either side can appeal a trial verdict if they believe the judge made legal errors that affected the outcome. Appeals courts don't retry cases or hear new evidence - they only review what happened during the original trial to determine if legal mistakes were made.

The appeals process has strict deadlines, typically requiring a Notice of Appeal to be filed within 30 to 60 days after the verdict. Appeals can take months or even years to resolve, and they're expensive and uncertain. Most personal injury appeals focus on issues like improper jury instructions, incorrectly admitted or excluded evidence, or procedural errors during trial.

## Understanding the Court Systems

**New York State Courts:** Personal injury lawsuits are filed in the Supreme Court of the county where your accident occurred. Don't let the name confuse you - New York's "Supreme Court" is actually the trial-level court for major civil cases. For smaller claims under $10,000 in New York City (or $5,000 elsewhere), you can use Small Claims Court, which offers a faster, less formal process.

**California State Courts:** Personal injury cases are filed in the Superior Court of the county where your accident happened. California's Superior Courts handle all civil cases regardless of the amount in dispute. For claims under $10,000, individuals can choose to use Small Claims Court, which provides a quicker resolution without the need for attorneys.

## Making Informed Decisions About Your Case

Understanding the litigation process empowers you to make smart decisions about your personal injury claim. Some cases truly need to go to trial to achieve fair compensation, while others are better resolved through negotiation or mediation. The key is having an experienced attorney who can evaluate your specific situation and guide you toward the best approach.

Remember that litigation is a marathon, not a sprint. The process can take months or years, and it requires patience, preparation, and persistence. However, for many injury victims, it's the only way to hold negligent parties accountable and obtain the compensation needed to rebuild their lives.

The decision to file a lawsuit shouldn't be taken lightly, but it shouldn't be feared either. With proper legal representation and a clear understanding of what lies ahead, you can navigate the litigation process with confidence, knowing that you're fighting for the justice and compensation you deserve.

## What Comes Next

In the following chapter, we'll dive deeper into the discovery process, exploring how depositions work, the role of expert witnesses, and specific strategies for preparing for trial. We'll also discuss how to work effectively with your attorney throughout the litigation process and what you can do to strengthen your case at each stage.

# 18

# Discovery and Pre-Trial Preparation

## *Gathering the Facts to Win Your Case*

After filing your personal injury lawsuit and completing the initial paperwork, your case enters one of its most important phases: discovery. This is where both sides dig deep to uncover the facts, gather evidence, and build their strongest possible arguments. Think of discovery as the investigation phase - it's where cases are often won or lost, and where many settlements are reached once the true strength of each side becomes clear.

### What Discovery Accomplishes

Discovery serves several crucial purposes in your case. It clarifies exactly what issues are in dispute, helps both sides understand the strengths and weaknesses of their positions, prevents surprise evidence from derailing your case at trial, and often facilitates settlement by revealing what evidence each party actually has. This transparency allows for more realistic settlement negotiations.

# The Discovery Toolkit

## Written Questions (Interrogatories)

These are formal written questions that one side sends to the other, and they must be answered under oath within 30 days. You might be asked about your background, exactly what happened during the incident, your complete medical history, and the financial losses you've suffered. While time-consuming, these questions help establish the basic facts of your case.

## Document Requests

Both sides can formally request relevant documents from each other. In personal injury cases, this typically includes all your medical records and bills, insurance policies and any communications with insurers, employment records and wage information, and any photographs, videos, or written statements related to your incident. These documents often provide the hard evidence needed to prove your case.

## Requests for Admissions

This tool helps narrow down what's actually in dispute. One side asks the other to admit or deny specific statements - if they're admitted, those facts are accepted as true for the rest of the case. This prevents wasting time at trial arguing over facts that aren't really contested.

## Depositions: The Power Tool

Depositions are live, recorded question-and-answer sessions conducted under oath, usually in a lawyer's office with a court reporter present. These are often the most revealing part of discovery. Depositions serve to lock in testimony so witnesses can't change their story later, evaluate how credible a witness will be at trial, and expose inconsistencies in someone's account of events.

If you're deposed, your attorney will prepare you beforehand. The key is to answer truthfully, stick to what you actually know, and not speculate or guess about things you're unsure of.

### Independent Medical Examinations (IMEs)

When your injuries are central to your case, the defense may request that you be examined by a doctor of their choosing. This can feel invasive, but it's a standard part of the process. Your attorney can attend the examination and object to any improper questioning. The doctor will write a report that becomes part of the case record.

## Expert Witnesses: The Specialists

Complex personal injury cases often require expert witnesses who can explain specialized topics to the jury. Medical experts explain the severity and long-term impact of your injuries, accident reconstruction specialists detail exactly how the incident occurred, vocational experts testify about how your injuries affect your ability to work, and economic experts project your future lost income and medical costs.

These experts submit detailed written reports during discovery and may be deposed or called to testify at trial. Good expert testimony can be crucial to proving the full extent of your damages.

## Pre-Trial Motions: Strategic Moves

Before trial begins, attorneys often file motions to shape how the case will proceed. A Motion to Compel Discovery is filed when the other side refuses to provide requested information. A Motion in Limine asks the judge to exclude prejudicial or irrelevant evidence that might unfairly influence the jury. A Motion for Summary Judgment asks the court to rule on part or all of the case based on facts that aren't in dispute, potentially avoiding trial altogether.

## Getting Ready for Trial

As your trial date approaches, your legal team engages in intensive preparation. They finalize the list of exhibits and witnesses, create detailed trial notebooks with all relevant information organized for quick reference, prepare you and other witnesses for testimony, develop compelling opening statements and closing arguments, and attend pre-trial conferences with the judge to resolve any remaining procedural issues.

In both New York and California, local court rules may require additional steps, such as mandatory mediation sessions or filing trial briefs that outline each side's legal arguments.

## The Strategic Importance

Discovery and pre-trial preparation form the foundation of every strong personal injury case. Through careful investigation, expert analysis, and strategic legal motions, both sides work to sharpen their arguments and clarify their positions. Cases that are well-prepared during this phase have significantly better outcomes, whether through favorable settlements or trial victories.

Being organized, responsive to your attorney's requests, and proactive during this phase greatly increases your chances of success. Many clients find that once discovery is complete and the evidence is laid out clearly, settlement negotiations become more productive as both sides have a realistic understanding of the case's strengths and weaknesses.

## What Comes Next

The thorough groundwork laid during discovery sets the stage for the final phases of your case: settlement negotiations, mediation, and potentially trial. With all the facts uncovered and evidence organized, you'll be in the strongest possible position to achieve a fair resolution, whether that happens at the negotiation table or in the courtroom.

19

# Negotiating a Settlement

*Getting a Fair Deal Without Going to Trial*

---

If you've been injured due to someone else's negligence, understanding the settlement process can mean the difference between fair compensation and leaving money on the table. Most personal injury cases - over 95% - settle out of court rather than going to trial. This comprehensive guide will walk you through everything you need to know about negotiating a fair settlement for your personal injury claim.

## Why Settlement Makes Sense

**Settlement Benefits:**

- **Speed**: Resolves your case in months rather than years
- **Certainty**: Guarantees compensation without trial risks
- **Cost-effective**: Avoids expensive court costs and extended legal fees
- **Privacy**: Keeps details of your case confidential
- **Less stress**: Eliminates the emotional toll of a lengthy court battle

**Trial Risks to Consider:**

- Unpredictable jury decisions
- No guarantee of winning
- Years of delays and appeals
- Substantial legal costs
- Public court records
- Emotional strain of testimony and cross-examination

## Understanding Settlement Timing

Settlement negotiations can happen at different stages of your case:

**Pre-Litigation (Before Filing Lawsuit):**

- Often occurs 3-6 months after your accident
- Best when liability is clear and injuries are well-documented
- Faster resolution but may result in lower offers

**During Litigation:**

- Happens after lawsuit is filed but before trial
- More leverage as insurers face trial costs
- Discovery process reveals stronger evidence

**Pre-Trial:**

- Occurs days or weeks before scheduled trial
- Highest settlement values due to trial pressure
- Both sides understand case strengths and weaknesses

**During Trial:**

- Can happen even after trial begins
- Rare but sometimes occurs when evidence is compelling

## Calculating Your Case Value

Before entering negotiations, understand what your case is worth by calculating both economic and non-economic damages:

### Economic Damages (Easy to Calculate)

**Medical Expenses:**

- Emergency room visits
- Hospital stays
- Doctor appointments
- Physical therapy
- Prescription medications
- Medical equipment (crutches, braces, etc.)
- Future medical care needs

**Lost Income:**

- Wages missed due to injury
- Sick time and vacation days used
- Reduced earning capacity
- Lost bonuses or overtime
- Business income if self-employed

**Out-of-Pocket Expenses:**

- Transportation to medical appointments
- Home modifications for disability
- Household help during recovery
- Childcare costs

### Non-Economic Damages (Harder to Calculate)

**Pain and Suffering:**

- Physical pain from injuries
- Ongoing discomfort
- Chronic pain conditions
- Sleep disruption

**Emotional Distress:**

- Anxiety and depression
- PTSD from the accident
- Loss of enjoyment of life
- Relationship strain

**Loss of Consortium:**

- Impact on marriage or family relationships
- Loss of companionship
- Inability to participate in family activities

## Calculating Pain and Suffering

Insurance companies typically use one of two methods:

**Multiplier Method:**

- Multiply economic damages by 1.5-5 depending on severity
- Minor injuries: 1.5-2x multiplier
- Moderate injuries: 2-3x multiplier
- Severe injuries: 3-5x multiplier

**Per Diem Method:**

- Assign daily dollar amount for pain and suffering
- Multiply by number of days affected
- Typically ranges from $50-$300 per day

# The Settlement Negotiation Process

## Step 1: Preparation

**Organize Your Documentation:**

- All medical records and bills
- Employment records showing lost wages
- Photos of injuries and accident scene
- Witness statements
- Police reports
- Insurance correspondence

**Set Your Bottom Line:**

- Determine minimum acceptable amount before negotiations begin
- Consider all damages, not just medical bills
- Factor in attorney fees if represented
- Don't share this number with the insurance company

## Step 2: The Demand Letter

Your demand letter is your opening statement in negotiations. A strong demand letter should include:

**Liability Section:**

- Clear explanation of how the accident happened
- Why the other party is at fault
- Supporting evidence (photos, witnesses, police report)

**Damages Section:**

- Itemized list of all medical expenses
- Documentation of lost wages

- Explanation of pain and suffering
- Future medical needs or limitations

**Demand Amount:**

- Start higher than your expected settlement
- Leave room for negotiation
- Justify the amount with evidence

**Professional Tone:**

- Stick to facts, avoid emotional language
- Be firm but respectful
- Include supporting documentation

## Step 3: Initial Offer and Response

**Expect a Lowball Offer:**

- First offers are typically 10-25% of your demand
- Don't take it personally - it's standard practice
- Use it as information about their negotiation strategy

**Analyze Their Response:**

- What damages are they disputing?
- Are they questioning liability?
- Do they challenge your medical treatment?
- Use their reasoning to craft your counteroffer

## Step 4: Making Strategic Counteroffers

**Counter-Offer Strategy:**

- Come down from your original demand, but not dramatically
- If you demanded $25,000 and they offered $5,000, counter at

$20,000-22,000

- Address their specific concerns with evidence
- Reaffirm liability and damages

**What to Include in Your Counter:**

- Response to their liability arguments
- Additional medical documentation if needed
- Clarification of treatment necessity
- Revised settlement amount with justification

### Step 5: Continued Negotiations

**Multiple Rounds Are Normal:**

- Expect 3-5 rounds of back-and-forth
- Each offer should move closer to middle ground
- Don't make dramatic drops in your demands

**Negotiation Psychology:**

- Insurance adjusters expect some negotiation
- Show flexibility but maintain your position on key points
- Document all conversations and offers

## When to Hold Firm vs. When to Compromise

### Hold Your Ground When:

**Strong Liability:**

- Clear evidence the other party is at fault
- Police report supports your version
- Witnesses back up your account

- Their insured admits fault

**Well-Documented Damages:**

- Complete medical records
- Clear connection between accident and injuries
- Treating physicians support your claims
- Objective evidence of pain and limitations

**Weak Insurance Arguments:**

- They can't provide evidence to support their position
- Their medical expert's opinion is questionable
- They're using generic databases rather than your actual treatment

## Consider Compromise When:

**Liability Questions Exist:**

- Shared fault in the accident
- Conflicting witness accounts
- No police report or unclear report
- Pre-existing injuries complicate your case

**Limited Long-term Impact:**

- Injuries have healed completely
- No ongoing treatment needed
- Return to normal activities
- Minimal lasting effects

**Practical Considerations:**

- Financial pressure to settle quickly
- Desire to avoid litigation stress
- Uncertainty about trial outcome

- Reasonable offer that covers most damages

## Red Flags in Settlement Negotiations

**Be Wary of:**

- Pressure to settle immediately
- Requests to sign documents before review
- Offers contingent on not consulting an attorney
- Settlement amounts that don't cover medical bills
- Vague language about what's being settled
- Requests for recorded statements after filing claim

## Alternative Dispute Resolution

### Mediation

**How It Works:**

- Neutral mediator facilitates discussion
- Parties remain in control of outcome
- Confidential process
- Non-binding unless agreement reached

**Benefits:**

- Less adversarial than litigation
- Often faster than court
- Maintains privacy
- Preserves relationships
- Creative solutions possible

**When to Consider:**

- Both parties want to settle but can't agree on amount
- Communication has broken down
- Complex cases with multiple issues
- Court-ordered mediation

## Arbitration

**How It Works:**

- Neutral arbitrator hears evidence
- More formal than mediation
- Decision can be binding or non-binding
- Limited appeal rights

**Types:**

- **Binding**: Final decision, limited appeal options
- **Non-binding**: Either party can reject and proceed to trial
- **High-low**: Parties agree on minimum and maximum award

**Considerations:**

- May be required by insurance policy
- Faster than trial but more formal than mediation
- Limited discovery process
- Arbitrator fees split between parties

# Settlement Documentation and Finalization

## Settlement Agreement Components

**Release of Liability:**

- You agree not to sue for this incident

- Covers the specific accident and injuries
- May include unknown injuries clause
- Sometimes covers related parties (employers, property owners)

**Payment Terms:**

- Total settlement amount
- Payment schedule (lump sum vs. installments)
- Timeline for payment (typically 30 days)
- What happens if payment is late

**Scope of Settlement:**

- What claims are being settled
- What parties are released
- Whether it covers future medical complications
- Workers' compensation liens and other claims

## Before Signing

**Review Carefully:**

- Understand every term in the agreement
- Ask questions about confusing language
- Ensure payment amount is correct
- Verify all parties are properly identified

**Consider Future Implications:**

- Will this cover future complications?
- Are you comfortable with the release language?
- Have all liens been identified and resolved?
- Do you understand tax implications?

## Lien Resolution

**Common Liens:**

- Health insurance subrogation claims
- Medicare/Medicaid liens
- Workers' compensation liens
- Hospital and doctor liens

**Your Attorney Should:**

- Identify all potential liens
- Negotiate reductions when possible
- Ensure proper payoff procedures
- Protect you from future lien claims

## Tax Implications of Settlements

**Generally Not Taxable:**

- Compensation for physical injuries
- Medical expense reimbursement
- Pain and suffering awards
- Emotional distress related to physical injury

**May Be Taxable:**

- Punitive damages (in some cases)
- Interest on delayed payments
- Lost wages portion (debated)
- Settlement for non-physical injuries

**Consult a Tax Professional:**

- Large settlements may have complex tax implications

- State tax laws may differ from federal
- Structured settlements have special rules
- Keep detailed records of settlement breakdown

## Common Settlement Mistakes to Avoid

**Settling Too Early:**

- Before understanding full extent of injuries
- Without completing medical treatment
- Under financial pressure
- Before getting legal advice

**Accepting Inadequate Offers:**

- Only covering medical bills
- Not accounting for pain and suffering
- Ignoring future medical needs
- Undervaluing lost wages

**Poor Documentation:**

- Incomplete medical records
- Missing wage information
- Lack of accident scene evidence
- No witness contact information

**Negotiation Errors:**

- Accepting first offer
- Making dramatic concessions
- Not understanding insurance tactics
- Failing to justify demands

## When to Hire an Attorney

**Consider Legal Representation When:**

- Injuries are serious or permanent
- Liability is disputed
- Multiple parties are involved
- Insurance company is uncooperative
- Settlement offers seem inadequate
- You're uncomfortable negotiating

**Benefits of Attorney Representation:**

- Knowledge of case values
- Experience with insurance tactics
- Resources for investigation
- Trial capability if needed
- Lien resolution expertise
- Peace of mind

**Attorney Fee Structures:**

- **Contingency**: Pay only if you win (typically 33-40%)
- **Hourly**: Pay for time spent regardless of outcome
- **Flat fee**: Rare in personal injury cases
- **Hybrid**: Combination of methods

## Red Flags: When Settlement May Not Be Right

**Consider Litigation When:**

- Insurance company is acting in bad faith
- Offers are unreasonably low despite strong case

- Liability is clear but insurer won't accept responsibility
- Serious injuries justify maximum compensation
- Multiple defendants complicate settlement
- Principle matters more than quick resolution

## Final Checklist Before Settling

**Before Accepting Any Settlement:**

✓ You've reached maximum medical improvement

✓ All medical bills have been identified

✓ Lost wages are fully calculated

✓ Future medical needs are considered

✓ Pain and suffering is fairly valued

✓ You understand what you're releasing

✓ All liens have been identified

✓ Payment terms are acceptable

✓ You're comfortable with the amount

✓ You've considered tax implications

## Conclusion

Settlement negotiation is both an art and a science. Success requires preparation, patience, and a clear understanding of your case's value. While the process can feel overwhelming, especially when you're recovering from injuries, a strategic approach to settlement can provide fair compensation without the uncertainty and stress of trial.

Remember that settlement is about finding a resolution that allows you to move forward with your life. The "perfect" settlement rarely exists, but a fair settlement should adequately compensate you for your injuries and losses while providing the certainty and closure you need to heal and rebuild.

Whether you choose to represent yourself or hire an attorney, understanding the settlement process empowers you to make informed decisions about your case. Take your time, document everything, and don't be afraid to ask questions. Your future financial security may depend on the decisions you make during these negotiations.

# 20

# Going to Trial

## *What To Expect if Your Case Goes to Court*

---

When most people think about personal injury cases, they imagine dramatic courtroom scenes from movies and TV shows. The reality is that the vast majority of personal injury cases - around 95% - settle out of court through negotiations between attorneys. However, when settlement talks break down or when the stakes are too high to compromise, your case may need to go to trial.

Understanding the trial process can help you feel more prepared and confident if your case heads to court. This comprehensive guide walks you through everything you need to know about personal injury trials, from the initial decision to go to trial through the final verdict and potential appeals.

## When Your Case Will Go to Trial

Several situations can lead to your personal injury case going to trial rather than settling out of court:

**The defendant completely denies they were at fault.** In some cases, the other party or their insurance company refuses to accept any responsibility for the accident that caused your injuries. They may claim the accident never happened, that someone else was responsible, or that their insured person did nothing wrong. When liability is contested this strongly, a trial may be necessary to let a judge or jury decide who was really at fault.

**You and the defendant can't agree on how much your case is worth.** Even when the other side admits they were at fault, they might offer far less money than what your injuries and damages are actually worth. If the gap between what you're asking for and what they're offering is too large to bridge through negotiations, a trial might be the only way to get fair compensation.

**Settlement negotiations completely break down.** Sometimes, despite everyone's best efforts, the parties simply can't reach an agreement. This might happen because of personality conflicts between the attorneys, unreasonable demands from either side, or fundamental disagreements about the facts of the case.

**Mediation fails to produce a settlement.** Many courts require parties to try mediation - a process where a neutral third party helps facilitate settlement discussions - before allowing a case to go to trial. If mediation doesn't result in an agreement, trial becomes the next step.

**Your attorney believes a trial will result in a better outcome.** In some cases, your lawyer might recommend going to trial because they believe a jury will award you more money than what's being offered in settlement negotiations. This might happen when your injuries are particularly severe, when the defendant's conduct was especially egregious, or when your case has strong emotional appeal that would resonate with a jury.

**The defendant's insurance company is being unreasonable.** Insurance companies sometimes take hardline positions and refuse to make fair settlement offers, betting that you won't want to go through the time, expense, and uncertainty of a trial. In these situations, actually going to trial can be the only way to get the insurance company to pay what your case is truly worth.

## Preparing for Trial: What You and Your Attorney Will Do

Going to trial requires months of intensive preparation. Your legal team will work tirelessly to build the strongest possible case, while you'll need to prepare yourself mentally and practically for the courtroom experience.

### Your Attorney's Trial Preparation

**Gathering and organizing all evidence.** Your lawyer will compile every piece of evidence that supports your case, including medical records, accident reports, photographs, witness statements, expert reports, and any other documentation that helps prove the defendant was at fault and that you suffered damages as a result.

**Preparing exhibits for court.** All evidence must be properly formatted and organized for presentation to the judge and jury. This might include creating enlarged photographs, charts, timelines, medical illustrations, or computer animations that help explain what happened and how you were injured.

**Finalizing the witness list.** Your attorney will determine which witnesses to call at trial, including you, any eyewitnesses to the accident, medical professionals who treated you, expert witnesses who can explain technical aspects of your case, and anyone else whose testimony supports your claims.

**Preparing opening and closing statements.** Your lawyer will craft compelling opening and closing arguments that tell your story in a clear, persuasive way. The opening statement gives the jury a roadmap of what evidence they'll see, while the closing argument ties everything together and asks the jury to rule in your favor.

**Developing your case narrative.** Every successful trial tells a story. Your attorney will work to present your case as a coherent narrative that shows how the defendant's negligence or wrongdoing caused your injuries and changed your life.

**Conducting practice sessions.** Many attorneys conduct mock trials or practice sessions where they present their case to a focus group or colleagues to identify weaknesses and refine their arguments.

**Preparing for cross-examination.** Your lawyer will anticipate the defense's arguments and prepare to challenge their witnesses and evidence through effective cross-examination.

**Researching legal precedents.** Your attorney will research similar cases and legal rulings that support your position, preparing legal arguments for any issues that might arise during trial.

## Your Preparation as the Plaintiff

**Learning to testify effectively.** You'll likely spend considerable time with your attorney practicing your testimony. This includes learning how to clearly explain what happened, how your injuries have affected your life, and how to answer questions from both your lawyer and the defense attorney.

**Understanding the courtroom process.** Your lawyer will explain courtroom procedures, what to expect each day of trial, how to dress and behave in court, and what the different phases of the trial will involve.

**Preparing for cross-examination.** The defense attorney will have the opportunity to question you, and their goal will be to poke holes in your story or minimize your damages. Your lawyer will help you prepare for potentially difficult or hostile questioning by practicing likely scenarios.

**Organizing your thoughts and memories.** You may need to testify about events that happened months or even years ago. Your attorney will help you review the facts of your case and organize your recollections so you can testify clearly and consistently.

**Preparing emotionally for the trial experience.** Trials can be stressful, emotionally draining, and sometimes confrontational. Your lawyer will help you understand what to expect and develop strategies for staying calm and composed under pressure.

**Gathering personal impact evidence.** You may need to provide testimony or documentation about how your injuries have affected your daily life, your relationships, your ability to work, and your overall quality of life.

## The Jury Selection Process (Voir Dire)

If your case will be decided by a jury rather than a judge alone, the trial begins with jury selection, also called "voir dire" (pronounced "vwar deer," which means "to speak the truth" in French). This process is crucial because the jurors who are selected will ultimately decide your case.

### How Jury Selection Works

**The jury pool is assembled.** The court summons a large group of potential jurors from voter registration lists, driver's license records, and other sources. These citizens are required by law to appear for jury duty.

**Initial screening.** The judge asks basic questions to identify people who can't serve due to hardship, scheduling conflicts, or other legitimate reasons. Some potential jurors may be excused at this stage.

**Questioning by attorneys.** Both your attorney and the defense attorney have the opportunity to ask potential jurors questions to learn about their backgrounds, experiences, opinions, and potential biases that might affect their ability to fairly decide your case.

**Identifying bias or prejudice.** The attorneys are looking for any indications that a potential juror might be unable to fairly consider the evidence. For example, a potential juror who has strong negative feelings about personal injury lawsuits, or who has had experiences that might make them sympathetic to one side or the other.

**Challenges for cause.** If a potential juror demonstrates clear bias or an inability to be fair, either attorney can ask the judge to dismiss that person "for cause." There's no limit to the number of for-cause challenges.

**Peremptory challenges.** Each side also gets a limited number of "peremptory challenges," which allow them to dismiss potential jurors without giving a reason. The number of peremptory challenges varies by jurisdiction but is typically between 3-6 per side.

## What Attorneys Look For in Jurors

**Life experiences that might affect their perspective.** Attorneys want to understand how potential jurors' personal experiences might influence their view of your case. Someone who has been in a similar accident might be more sympathetic, while someone who has been sued might be more skeptical of personal injury claims.

**Attitudes toward personal injury lawsuits.** Some people have negative opinions about personal injury cases, believing that too many lawsuits are frivolous or that people are trying to get rich quick from accidents. These individuals might not be fair jurors in your case.

**Ability to award appropriate damages.** Some potential jurors might be uncomfortable awarding large sums of money for pain and suffering, even when it's justified. Attorneys need jurors who can fairly evaluate all types of damages.

**Communication and leadership styles.** Attorneys pay attention to how potential jurors interact with others and express themselves, as these individuals will need to deliberate together to reach a verdict.

## The Phases of Your Trial

Once the jury is selected, your trial will proceed through several distinct phases. Understanding each phase helps you know what to expect and when you might be called upon to participate.

### Opening Statements

**Your attorney goes first.** As the plaintiff, your lawyer gets to present their opening statement before the defense. This is your attorney's opportunity to tell the jury what the case is about, what evidence they'll see, and what you're asking the jury to do.

**Setting expectations.** The opening statement isn't an argument - it's a preview of the evidence. Your lawyer will outline the key facts of your case, explain how the defendant's actions caused your injuries, and describe the impact those injuries have had on your life.

**The defense responds.** After your attorney's opening statement, the defense lawyer presents their version of events. They might dispute the facts, argue that their client wasn't at fault, or claim that your injuries aren't as serious as you say they are.

**First impressions matter.** Research shows that many jurors form initial opinions about a case based on the opening statements, so this phase is crucial for framing how the jury will view all the evidence that follows.

### Presenting Your Case (Plaintiff's Case-in-Chief)

**You present your evidence first.** As the plaintiff, you have the burden of proving your case, so you get to present your evidence before the defense presents theirs.

**Witness testimony.** Your attorney will call various witnesses to testify on your behalf. This typically includes:

- **You, the plaintiff:** You'll testify about how the accident happened, your injuries, your medical treatment, and how the injuries have affected your life.
- **Eyewitnesses:** People who saw the accident happen can testify about what they observed.

- **Medical providers:** Doctors, nurses, therapists, and other healthcare providers who treated you will testify about your injuries, treatment, and prognosis.

- **Expert witnesses:** Specialists such as accident reconstruction experts, medical experts, economists, or vocational rehabilitation experts may testify to help explain technical aspects of your case.

- **Family and friends:** People close to you might testify about how your injuries have changed your life and relationships.

**Physical evidence and exhibits.** Your attorney will present photographs, medical records, bills, employment records, and any other physical evidence that supports your case.

**Building your story piece by piece.** Each witness and piece of evidence adds another element to the overall story of what happened to you and why you deserve compensation.

## The Defense's Case

**The defense gets their turn.** After you've presented all your evidence, the defense has the opportunity to present their case. They might call their own witnesses and present evidence that contradicts your claims or minimizes your damages.

**Common defense strategies include:**

- **Disputing fault:** Arguing that their client wasn't responsible for the accident or that you were partially or entirely at fault.

- **Minimizing injuries:** Claiming that your injuries aren't as serious as you claim, that they were pre-existing, or that they were caused by something other than the accident.

- **Challenging damages:** Arguing that you're asking for too much money or that certain expenses aren't related to the accident.

- **Presenting alternative explanations:** Offering different versions of how the accident happened or what caused your injuries.

**Defense witnesses might include:**

- **The defendant:** The person or company you're suing may testify in their own defense.

- **Defense medical experts:** Doctors hired by the defense who may disagree with your doctors' opinions about your injuries or treatment.
- **Other eyewitnesses:** People who saw the accident and have a different recollection of what happened.
- **Expert witnesses:** Specialists who support the defense's version of events or conclusions.

## Cross-Examination

**Both sides get to challenge witnesses.** After each witness testifies for the side that called them (called "direct examination"), the opposing attorney gets to cross-examine them.

**The purpose of cross-examination.** Cross-examination is designed to challenge the witness's testimony, expose inconsistencies, raise doubts about their credibility, or get them to admit facts that help the other side's case.

**What to expect when you're cross-examined.** The defense attorney may:

- Ask you about inconsistencies between your testimony and previous statements
- Question you about your medical history or pre-existing conditions
- Challenge your recollection of events
- Ask about your financial situation or motivation for filing the lawsuit
- Try to minimize the impact of your injuries on your life

**Staying calm during cross-examination.** Cross-examination can feel confrontational, but remember that the defense attorney is just doing their job. Listen carefully to each question, take your time answering, and tell the truth. If you don't know or don't remember something, it's okay to say so.

## Rebuttal Evidence

**Responding to the defense's case.** After the defense presents their case, you may have the opportunity to present rebuttal evidence that responds to or contradicts what the defense presented.

**Limited scope.** Rebuttal evidence must relate to something the defense brought up - you can't present entirely new claims or evidence that you should have included in your original case.

## Closing Arguments

**Your final opportunity to persuade the jury.** Closing arguments are each side's last chance to speak directly to the jury before they begin deliberating.

**Your attorney's closing argument.** Your lawyer will:

- Summarize the evidence that supports your case
- Explain why the defendant should be held responsible
- Describe the full extent of your damages and explain why you deserve the compensation you're asking for
- Address any weaknesses in your case or arguments made by the defense
- Make an emotional appeal for justice

**The defense's closing argument.** The defense attorney will argue why their client shouldn't be held responsible or why you shouldn't receive the compensation you're asking for.

**Rebuttal closing.** Since you have the burden of proof, your attorney gets the last word with a brief rebuttal that responds to the defense's closing argument.

## Jury Instructions

**The judge explains the law.** Before the jury begins deliberating, the judge will provide them with detailed instructions about the legal standards they must apply when deciding your case.

**Key instructions typically include:**

- The burden of proof (preponderance of the evidence in civil cases)
- The legal definition of negligence or other theories of liability
- What types of damages can be awarded

- How to calculate different types of damages
- Any special legal rules that apply to your type of case

**Both sides may propose instructions.** Your attorney and the defense attorney can suggest specific jury instructions, and the judge decides which ones to give.

## Jury Deliberation and Reaching a Verdict

**Private deliberations.** After receiving their instructions, the jury retires to a private room to discuss the case and reach a verdict. No one else is allowed in the deliberation room, and the discussions are confidential.

**Selecting a foreperson.** The jury will select one member to serve as the foreperson, who leads discussions and communicates with the court.

**Reviewing evidence.** The jury can ask to review specific pieces of evidence, re-read testimony, or have the judge clarify legal instructions.

**Reaching a decision.** In most civil cases, the jury doesn't need to be unanimous - typically, a majority of jurors (such as 9 out of 12) can reach a verdict.

**The verdict form.** The jury will complete a verdict form that indicates:

- Whether they find the defendant liable (responsible) for your injuries
- If so, how much money you should be awarded for various types of damages
- In some cases, whether you were partially at fault and, if so, what percentage of fault to assign to you

**Returning to court.** When the jury reaches a verdict, everyone returns to the courtroom for the reading of the verdict.

## Understanding Bench Trials

**When a judge decides your case.** In some situations, your case might be decided by a judge alone rather than a jury. This is called a "bench trial."

**When bench trials occur:**

- Either you or the defendant requests a bench trial instead of a jury trial
- The amount of money involved is below the threshold for a jury trial in your jurisdiction
- Both sides agree that the issues are primarily legal rather than factual
- The type of case typically doesn't involve jury trials

**Advantages of bench trials:**

- **Faster resolution:** Bench trials typically take less time than jury trials
- **Less formal atmosphere:** The proceedings may be somewhat less formal and intimidating
- **Predictable decision-maker:** Judges are experienced in evaluating evidence and applying the law
- **No jury selection:** You skip the time-consuming voir dire process
- **Focus on legal issues:** Judges are less likely to be swayed by emotional appeals and more focused on the legal merits

**Disadvantages of bench trials:**

- **No jury sympathy:** You lose the potential for a jury to be moved by your story and award significant damages for pain and suffering
- **Single decision-maker:** All the power rests with one person rather than a group of your peers
- **Judge's biases:** Individual judges may have particular views about personal injury cases that could work against you

## The Burden of Proof in Civil Cases

**What you must prove.** As the plaintiff in a personal injury case, you have the "burden of proof," which means you must convince the judge or jury that your version of events is correct.

**Preponderance of the evidence standard.** In civil cases, you must prove your case by a "preponderance of the evidence." This means that it's more likely than not (greater than 50% probability) that:

- The defendant was negligent or otherwise at fault
- The defendant's actions caused your injuries
- You suffered damages as a result

**Lower standard than criminal cases.** This is a much lower standard than in criminal cases, where guilt must be proven "beyond a reasonable doubt." You don't need to prove your case with absolute certainty - just that your version is more likely to be true than the defendant's version.

**Elements you must prove:**

- **Duty:** The defendant owed you a duty of care
- **Breach:** The defendant breached that duty through their actions or inactions
- **Causation:** The defendant's breach of duty caused your injuries
- **Damages:** You suffered actual harm as a result

## What Happens After the Verdict

### If You Win Your Case

**Monetary award.** If the jury or judge rules in your favor, you'll be awarded monetary damages. This might include:

- **Economic damages:** Medical expenses, lost wages, future medical costs, future lost earning capacity
- **Non-economic damages:** Pain and suffering, emotional distress, loss of enjoyment of life
- **Punitive damages:** In rare cases involving particularly egregious conduct, additional damages designed to punish the defendant

**Written judgment.** The court will enter a written judgment that officially records the verdict and the amount of money you're owed.

**Collecting your money.** Unfortunately, winning a judgment doesn't automatically mean you'll get paid immediately. The defendant or their insurance company may need time to arrange payment, or there may be disputes about the amount owed.

## If You Lose Your Case

**No compensation.** If the jury or judge rules against you, you won't receive any compensation for your injuries and damages.

**Potential cost responsibility.** Depending on your jurisdiction and the specific circumstances of your case, you might be responsible for paying some of the defendant's court costs (though typically not their attorney fees in personal injury cases).

**Consider an appeal.** If you believe legal errors affected the outcome of your trial, you may have grounds to appeal the decision to a higher court.

# Post-Trial Motions and Appeals

## Post-Trial Motions

**Motion for a new trial.** Either side can ask the judge to order a new trial if they believe significant errors occurred during the trial that affected the outcome. Common grounds include:

- Jury misconduct
- Significant errors in jury instructions
- Improper admission or exclusion of evidence
- Attorney misconduct

**Motion for judgment notwithstanding the verdict (JNOV).** This motion asks the judge to overturn the jury's verdict because no reasonable jury could have reached that conclusion based on the evidence presented.

**Motion to alter or amend judgment.** This motion asks the court to change some aspect of the judgment, such as the amount of damages awarded.

**Timing.** These motions must typically be filed within a specific time period after the verdict, often within 30 days.

## The Appeals Process

**Grounds for appeal.** Appeals focus on legal errors, not factual disputes. You can't appeal just because you disagree with the jury's verdict - you must show that the judge made legal mistakes that affected the outcome.

**Common grounds for appeal include:**

- Incorrect jury instructions
- Improper admission or exclusion of evidence
- Errors in applying the law
- Procedural mistakes that affected the fairness of the trial

**Filing deadlines.** Appeals must be filed within strict deadlines:

- **New York:** Generally 30 days from entry of judgment
- **California:** Generally 60 days from entry of judgment
- **Federal court:** Generally 30 days from entry of judgment

**The appellate process:**

- **Notice of appeal:** You must file a formal notice that you're appealing the decision
- **Record preparation:** The court reporter prepares a written transcript of the trial proceedings
- **Briefs:** Both sides submit written arguments explaining their legal positions
- **Oral argument:** In some cases, attorneys present their arguments to the appellate judges
- **Decision:** The appellate court issues a written decision

**Possible outcomes of an appeal:**

- **Affirmed:** The appellate court agrees with the trial court's decision
- **Reversed:** The appellate court disagrees and changes the outcome
- **Remanded:** The appellate court sends the case back to the trial court for further proceedings, such as a new trial

**Appeals take time.** The appeals process can take anywhere from several months to several years to complete.

# Emotional and Practical Considerations

## Preparing Yourself Mentally

**Trials are stressful.** Even with the best preparation, going to trial can be one of the most stressful experiences of your life. You'll be discussing traumatic events, facing cross-examination, and having your credibility questioned in a public forum.

**The process is unpredictable.** Unlike settlement negotiations, where you have some control over the outcome, trials involve many variables you can't control, including the personalities of individual jurors, unexpected testimony, and the judge's rulings on evidence.

**Trials take time.** Personal injury trials can last anywhere from a few days to several weeks, depending on the complexity of the case. You'll need to be available for the entire trial, which may require taking time off work.

**Public proceedings.** Trials are generally open to the public, which means that anyone can attend and listen to the details of your case. This can feel invasive, especially when discussing personal medical information or the impact of your injuries on your life.

## Practical Considerations

**Court schedules can be unpredictable.** Trials are frequently delayed or rescheduled due to the court's calendar, emergencies with other cases, or unexpected developments. You'll need to be flexible with your schedule.

**Dress and behavior expectations.** Courts have strict expectations about appropriate dress and behavior. Your attorney will provide guidance on what to wear and how to conduct yourself in the courtroom.

**Facing the defendant.** You'll likely have to sit in the same courtroom as the person or company you're suing, which can be emotionally difficult, especially if the defendant was responsible for a traumatic accident.

**Media attention.** Depending on the nature of your case, there might be media interest in your trial. Your attorney can help you prepare for this possibility and develop strategies for dealing with reporters.

### The Empowering Aspects of Trial

**Having your day in court.** For many people, the opportunity to tell their story in a formal legal proceeding and seek justice through the court system can be empowering and provide a sense of closure.

**Holding defendants accountable.** Trials can serve an important function in holding negligent parties accountable for their actions and potentially preventing similar harm to others in the future.

**Vindicating your position.** A favorable verdict can provide validation that you were right to pursue your case and that your injuries and damages were real and significant.

**Setting precedent.** Your case might establish legal precedents or result in policy changes that benefit others in similar situations.

## Making the Decision: Trial vs. Settlement

### Factors to Consider

**Strength of your case.** Cases with clear liability and well-documented damages are more likely to succeed at trial, while cases with disputed facts or questionable damages might be better candidates for settlement.

**Amount at stake.** If the settlement offers are far below what your case is worth, trial might be worth the risk. However, if the settlement offer is reasonable, it might make sense to accept the certainty of settlement rather than risk an unfavorable verdict at trial.

**Your personal circumstances.** Consider your health, financial situation, and emotional capacity to handle the stress and time commitment of a trial.

**The defendant's resources.** There's no point in winning a large judgment if the defendant doesn't have the money or insurance coverage to pay it.

**Your attorney's recommendation.** Your lawyer has experience evaluating cases and can provide valuable guidance about whether your case is likely to succeed at trial.

## Questions to Discuss with Your Attorney

- What are the strengths and weaknesses of our case?
- What's the range of potential outcomes if we go to trial?
- How long is the trial likely to take?
- What are the estimated costs of going to trial?
- What settlement offers have been made, and are they reasonable?
- What's your success rate with similar cases that have gone to trial?
- What are the risks of an unfavorable verdict?

# Conclusion

Going to trial in a personal injury case is a significant decision that shouldn't be taken lightly. While the process can be stressful, time-consuming, and unpredictable, it also offers the opportunity for a full and fair resolution when settlement negotiations fail.

The key to a successful trial experience is thorough preparation, realistic expectations, and strong communication with your attorney throughout the process. Understanding what to expect at each stage of the trial can help reduce anxiety and allow you to participate more effectively in your own case.

Remember that the decision to go to trial should be based on a careful evaluation of your specific circumstances, the strength of your case, and your personal goals. With the right preparation and legal representation, a trial can be an empowering experience that results in the justice and compensation you deserve.

Whether your case settles or goes to trial, the most important thing is that you receive fair compensation for your injuries and that those responsible for your harm are held accountable for their actions. Your attorney is your advocate throughout this process, working to achieve the best possible outcome for your unique situation.

# 21

# Calculating and Receiving Compensation

## *When and How You'll Get Paid*

Congratulations on reaching a successful resolution to your personal injury case. Whether through settlement or trial verdict, you've achieved an important milestone in your recovery journey. Now comes the next crucial phase: understanding exactly how your compensation works and what to expect when those funds arrive.

Many clients find themselves with questions after their case concludes. How exactly are damages calculated? What's the difference between economic and non-economic damages? Will you receive your money all at once or over time? What deductions should you expect? This comprehensive guide answers these questions and prepares you for the final steps of your legal journey.

### The Three Types of Compensation You May Receive

Personal injury awards typically fall into three distinct categories, each serving a different purpose in making you whole again.

## Economic Damages: Your Out-of-Pocket Recovery

Economic damages represent the most straightforward component of your award. These are the tangible, measurable expenses you've incurred or will incur as a direct result of your injury. Think of these as the bills and financial losses you can document with receipts, invoices, and pay stubs.

**Medical expenses** form the largest portion of most economic damage awards. This includes not only the emergency room visit, surgery, or initial treatment you received immediately after your accident, but also ongoing medical care. Physical therapy sessions, follow-up appointments with specialists, prescription medications, medical equipment like wheelchairs or braces, and even future medical procedures your doctor says you'll need are all part of this calculation.

**Lost wages** compensate you for the income you've already missed due to your injury, while **lost earning capacity** addresses your reduced ability to earn money in the future. If your injury prevents you from returning to your previous job or limits your career advancement, this component ensures you're compensated for that long-term financial impact.

**Property damage** covers repair or replacement of items damaged in your accident, most commonly your vehicle. **Transportation costs** for medical appointments, **rehabilitation expenses**, and **home modifications** needed to accommodate your injury round out the economic damages category.

## Non-Economic Damages: Compensating Life's Intangible Losses

While economic damages are relatively easy to calculate, non-economic damages address the ways your injury has affected your quality of life. These losses are real and significant, even though they don't come with a receipt or invoice.

**Pain and suffering** represents the physical discomfort and emotional anguish you've experienced since your accident. This includes not only the immediate pain from your injury but also ongoing discomfort, the frustration of lengthy recovery periods, and the anxiety many people feel about their condition.

**Emotional distress** encompasses depression, anxiety, sleep disturbances, and other psychological impacts of your injury. Many accident victims find themselves afraid to drive, anxious in crowds, or struggling with mood changes they never experienced before their accident.

**Loss of enjoyment of life** compensates you for activities you can no longer participate in or enjoy as you once did. If you were an avid runner who can no longer jog due to a knee injury, or if chronic pain prevents you from playing with your children the way you used to, this component addresses those losses.

**Loss of consortium** affects your relationship with your spouse or family members, compensating for the ways your injury has impacted your ability to provide companionship, affection, and support to your loved ones.

Calculating non-economic damages requires more subjective judgment than economic damages. Courts and insurance companies typically use one of two methods: the **multiplier method**, where economic damages are multiplied by a factor between 1.5 and 5 depending on the severity of your injuries, or the **per diem method**, which assigns a daily dollar amount to your suffering and multiplies it by the number of days you've been affected.

### Punitive Damages: When the Focus Shifts to Punishment

Punitive damages serve a different purpose entirely. Rather than compensating you for your losses, they're designed to punish defendants who acted with gross negligence or intentional misconduct and to deter others from similar behavior.

These damages are relatively rare in personal injury cases and are more likely to be awarded in certain jurisdictions. California courts are generally more receptive to punitive damage claims, while New York strictly limits when they can be awarded. Your attorney can explain whether punitive damages might apply to your specific case and jurisdiction.

## How You'll Receive Your Compensation

Once your compensation amount is determined, the next question becomes how and when you'll receive those funds. There are two primary methods of payment, each with distinct advantages and considerations.

## Lump-Sum Payments: Immediate Access to Your Award

The vast majority of personal injury settlements and judgments are paid as lump sums. This means you receive the entire compensation amount in a single payment, typically within 30 days of finalizing your settlement agreement or receiving a judgment.

Lump-sum payments offer maximum flexibility. You have immediate access to funds for medical bills, living expenses, or investments. You can pay off debts, make major purchases, or set aside money for future needs according to your own priorities and timeline.

This method works well for smaller settlements or cases where you have immediate financial needs that require a large payment. It also provides certainty - you know exactly how much you're receiving and when.

## Structured Settlements: Guaranteed Income Over Time

Structured settlements involve receiving your compensation through a series of payments over months, years, or even decades. Instead of one large payment, you receive a predictable income stream through an annuity purchased from a highly-rated insurance company.

These arrangements are particularly common in cases involving substantial awards, injuries to minors, or individuals with long-term disabilities who will need ongoing care and support. The payment schedule can be customized to your needs - you might receive larger payments initially to cover immediate expenses, followed by smaller regular payments, or payments that increase over time to account for inflation.

**The advantages of structured settlements** include tax benefits, since the growth of your annuity funds is tax-free. You're also protected against the temptation or pressure to spend a large sum quickly, ensuring long-term financial security. The guaranteed payments continue regardless of market conditions or economic downturns.

**The primary drawback** is reduced flexibility. Once established, structured settlements are difficult and expensive to modify. If you face an unexpected financial emergency, you can't simply withdraw additional funds from your settlement. Some companies offer to purchase structured settlement rights for immediate cash, but these transactions typically provide significantly less than the full value of your future payments.

Your attorney can help you evaluate whether a structured settlement makes sense for your situation and assist in negotiating terms with a reputable annuity provider if you choose this option.

## Understanding Deductions from Your Award

Before you receive your portion of the settlement or judgment, several deductions may reduce the final amount that reaches your bank account. Understanding these deductions helps you plan realistically for your financial future.

### Attorney's Fees

If your attorney represented you on a contingency fee basis - meaning they only get paid if you win - their percentage comes out of your award first. Contingency fees typically range from 25% to 40% of your gross settlement, with the exact percentage depending on factors like the complexity of your case, whether it settled before trial, and the terms of your retainer agreement.

This fee structure means your attorney shared the risk of your case with you. They invested their time, expertise, and resources with no guarantee of payment, only collecting a fee when they successfully obtained compensation for you.

### Case Costs and Expenses

Throughout your case, your attorney likely advanced various costs on your behalf. These **case costs** are separate from attorney's fees and are typically reimbursed from your settlement. Common expenses include court filing fees, costs for obtaining medical records, expert witness fees, deposition expenses, investigation costs, and trial exhibits or demonstrative aids.

Reputable attorneys provide detailed accounting of these expenses, and many work to minimize costs where possible while still building the strongest possible case for you.

### Medical Liens: Repaying Those Who Treated You

**Medical liens** represent one of the most complex aspects of settlement distribution. When you receive medical treatment after an accident, healthcare providers, insurance companies, and government programs often agree to wait for payment until your case resolves, knowing they'll be reimbursed from your settlement.

**Health insurance liens** arise when your health insurance paid for accident-related medical care. Your insurance company typically has a contractual right to be reimbursed from your settlement for these payments. However, experienced attorneys can often negotiate significant reductions in these liens, particularly when the full lien amount would consume a disproportionate share of your settlement.

**Hospital and provider liens** occur when hospitals or doctors provide treatment and agree to wait for payment from your settlement. These liens must be satisfied before you receive your portion of the award.

**Government program liens** are among the most complex. Medicare, Medicaid (called Medi-Cal in California), and the Veterans Administration have statutory rights to reimbursement from personal injury settlements. These liens often require careful legal analysis and negotiation to ensure compliance with federal regulations while minimizing the impact on your recovery.

**Workers' compensation liens** may apply if you were injured at work and received workers' compensation benefits while also pursuing a third-party personal injury claim.

An experienced attorney plays a crucial role in identifying all potential liens, negotiating reductions where possible, and ensuring that lien holders are paid appropriately while maximizing your final recovery.

## Timeline: When to Expect Your Funds

The timeline for receiving your compensation varies depending on several factors, but understanding typical timeframes helps you plan accordingly.

### Settlement Payments

For resolved settlements, you can typically expect to receive your funds within 30 to 60 days after signing the final release agreement. This timeframe allows for:

- Processing of the settlement paperwork

- Resolution of any outstanding liens
- Transfer of funds from the defendant's insurance company
- Distribution calculations and final accounting
- Cutting and mailing of settlement checks

## Judgment Payments

If your case went to trial and resulted in a judgment in your favor, the timeline may be longer. Defendants often file post-trial motions or appeals, which can delay payment for months or even years. However, in many jurisdictions, judgment creditors can begin collection efforts immediately, and defendants may choose to pay promptly to avoid accumulating interest on the judgment.

## Structured Settlement Payments

If you've chosen a structured settlement, your first payment will typically arrive on a predetermined date specified in your settlement agreement, often 30 to 90 days after finalizing the arrangement. Subsequent payments follow the schedule outlined in your annuity contract.

## Common Causes of Delays

Several factors can extend these timelines:

**Lien disputes** arise when there's disagreement about the amount or validity of claimed liens. Resolving these disputes may require negotiation or court intervention.

**Multiple defendants** can complicate settlement distribution, particularly when different defendants' insurance companies are involved or when there are disputes about each party's share of responsibility.

**Court approval requirements** apply in cases involving minors, individuals with certain disabilities, or settlements that exceed specific dollar thresholds. Courts review these settlements to ensure they're in the injured party's best interests, which adds time to the process.

**Complex settlement structures** or international defendants can also create additional processing time.

# Tax Implications: What You Need to Know

Understanding the tax implications of your personal injury settlement helps you plan effectively and avoid surprises at tax time.

## Generally Non-Taxable Compensation

Under federal tax law, compensation for physical personal injuries is typically not considered taxable income. This means the portion of your settlement compensating you for medical expenses, lost wages due to physical injury, pain and suffering related to physical injuries, and emotional distress directly related to physical injuries generally won't increase your tax liability.

This tax treatment recognizes that personal injury compensation is intended to make you whole rather than provide you with income or profit.

## Potentially Taxable Components

Certain portions of personal injury awards may be taxable:

**Punitive damages** are generally considered taxable income, since they're intended to punish the defendant rather than compensate you for losses.

**Interest on judgments** – the interest that accumulates on court judgments from the date of judgment until payment – is typically taxable as income.

**Emotional distress awards** may be taxable if they're not directly related to a physical injury. For example, if you received compensation solely for emotional distress without any physical injury component, that portion might be taxable.

**Lost wage compensation** maintains the same tax character as the wages you lost. If the lost wages would have been taxable income, the compensation for those wages may also be taxable.

## Planning Recommendations

Given the complexity of tax law and the significant amounts often involved in personal injury settlements, consulting with a qualified tax professional is strongly recommended. A tax advisor can help you:

- Understand the specific tax implications of your settlement

- Plan for any tax liabilities that may arise
- Structure your financial planning to minimize tax impact
- Ensure proper reporting on your tax returns

## Preparing for Life After Settlement

Receiving your personal injury compensation marks the end of your legal case but the beginning of a new chapter in your financial life. Whether you receive a lump sum or structured settlement, thoughtful planning helps ensure your compensation serves its intended purpose: providing financial security and helping you rebuild your life.

Consider your immediate needs first. Outstanding medical bills, living expenses during recovery, and necessary home or vehicle modifications should take priority. If you're receiving a lump sum, resist the pressure to make major financial decisions immediately. Many financial advisors recommend waiting several months to make significant investments or purchases, giving yourself time to adjust to your new circumstances.

For larger settlements, assembling a team of professional advisors - including a financial planner, tax professional, and estate planning attorney - can help you make the most of your compensation while protecting your long-term interests.

Remember that your personal injury settlement is designed to compensate you for losses and help you move forward. While no amount of money can fully compensate for serious injuries or their impact on your life, proper management of your settlement funds can provide security and opportunity for years to come.

Your legal journey may be concluding, but your recovery and your future continue. The compensation you've received represents not just acknowledgment of what you've endured, but investment in your path forward. Understanding how that compensation works - from calculation to payment to tax implications - empowers you to make informed decisions as you rebuild and move ahead.

In the next phase of your journey, you'll work with lien holders and manage the various deductions that affect your final payout. Armed with this understanding of how compensation works, you're better prepared to navigate those final steps and begin your new chapter with confidence and clarity.

# 22

# Handling Liens and Deductions

## *Making Sure You Keep as Much of Your Money as Possible*

**Bottom Line Up Front:** Liens can dramatically reduce your settlement payout, but with the right knowledge and negotiation strategies, you can minimize their impact and maximize your recovery.

## What This Guide Covers

If you've been injured and are expecting a settlement, you need to understand that various parties may have legal claims to portions of your money. This guide explains who can take money from your settlement, how much they can take, and most importantly - how to reduce what you owe them.

**Key Takeaway:** Most liens can be negotiated down significantly, potentially saving you thousands of dollars.

## Understanding Liens: The Basics

### What Exactly Is a Lien?

Think of a lien as an IOU that gets automatically attached to your settlement money. When someone provides medical care, insurance coverage, or other benefits related to your injury, they may gain the legal right to be repaid from any settlement or court award you receive.

**Important Note:** Liens must typically be satisfied before you can access your settlement funds. Your attorney cannot simply ignore them.

### Why Liens Exist

Liens prevent what lawyers call "double recovery" - the idea that you shouldn't profit from receiving both free medical care and settlement money for the same injury. While this sounds reasonable in theory, liens can sometimes leave injured people with surprisingly little money after everyone else gets paid.

## The Complete Guide to Lien Types

### 1. Medical Provider Liens: The Most Common Type

**Who Files Them:** Hospitals, emergency rooms, doctors, physical therapists, imaging centers, and other healthcare providers

**When They Apply:**

- You received treatment but couldn't pay upfront
- You signed a "Letter of Protection" or lien agreement
- The provider treated you knowing you had a pending injury case
- You were uninsured or underinsured at the time of treatment

**Real-World Example:** You're taken to the emergency room after a car accident. The hospital bill is $15,000, but you don't have insurance. The hospital may file a lien against any future settlement, expecting to be paid from your award.

**Negotiation Potential:** HIGH (25-60% reductions are common)

**Red Flags to Watch For:**

- Billing for services not related to your injury
- Duplicate charges for the same procedure
- Charges that seem excessive compared to standard rates
- Interest or collection fees added to medical bills

## 2. Health Insurance Subrogation: Your Insurer Wants Payback

**Who Files Them:** Private health insurance companies, employer health plans, union health funds

**How It Works:** Your health insurance paid for accident-related medical care upfront. Now they want to be reimbursed from your settlement because, technically, the at-fault party (not your insurance) should pay for accident-related medical expenses.

**What Your Policy Says:** Most health insurance policies contain "subrogation clauses" that give the insurer the right to recover payments from third-party settlements. You agreed to this when you signed up for coverage.

**Negotiation Strategies:**

- **Common Fund Doctrine:** Argue that your attorney's work benefited the insurance company by recovering money they otherwise wouldn't have gotten
- **Attorney Fee Sharing:** Many insurers will reduce their claim by 33% (the typical attorney fee percentage)
- **Proportionate Share:** If you didn't recover full compensation, the insurer should only recover proportionally

**Sample Negotiation:** If your insurer paid $10,000 in medical bills and you recovered $50,000 in a case worth $100,000, they should only recover $5,000 (50% of their claim).

## 3. Medicare Liens: Federal Law Requires Repayment

**Why Medicare Is Different:** Medicare is backed by federal law, making these liens more difficult to avoid or negotiate than private liens.

**The Process:**

1. **Conditional Payment Summary:** Medicare provides a list of all payments they made related to your injury
2. **Notification Requirement:** You must report your settlement to Medicare's Benefits Coordination & Recovery Center (BCRC)
3. **Final Demand:** Medicare calculates the final amount owed after considering attorney fees and costs
4. **120-Day Rule:** You have 120 days after settling to pay Medicare back

**Negotiation Opportunities:**

- **Pro-rata reduction** for attorney fees and case costs
- **Hardship waivers** in cases of financial need
- **Compromise amounts** in certain circumstances

**Common Mistake:** Failing to notify Medicare of a settlement can result in penalties and collection actions.

## 4. Medicaid (Medi-Cal) Liens: State-by-State Variations

**Key Legal Principle:** The Ahlborn rule limits Medicaid recovery to only the portion of your settlement that represents medical expenses, not pain and suffering or lost wages.

**How This Helps You:** If your $100,000 settlement breaks down as $30,000 for medical expenses and $70,000 for pain and suffering, Medicaid can only claim against the $30,000 medical portion.

**State-Specific Rules:** Each state handles Medicaid recovery differently. Some are aggressive, others rarely pursue small liens.

**Documentation Strategy:** Your attorney should prepare a detailed breakdown showing how much of your settlement represents medical expenses versus other damages.

## 5. ERISA Plan Liens: The Toughest to Fight

**What ERISA Means:** The Employee Retirement Income Security Act governs most employer-sponsored health plans.

**Why They're Difficult:** ERISA plans often have very strong subrogation language and are governed by federal law, limiting your ability to negotiate.

**Special Considerations:**

- ERISA plans may claim the right to recover their full payment regardless of your attorney fees
- Some courts have ruled that the "common fund doctrine" doesn't apply to ERISA plans
- These liens often cannot be discharged in bankruptcy

**Strategy:** Focus on challenging the validity of claimed expenses rather than negotiating percentage reductions.

### 6. Workers' Compensation Liens: When Work and Personal Injury Overlap

**Common Scenario:** You're injured in a car accident while driving for work. You receive workers' comp benefits, but you also have a personal injury claim against the other driver.

**Dual Recovery Rules:** Workers' comp insurers have the right to recover their payments from third-party settlements to prevent you from being paid twice for the same injury.

**Negotiation Factors:**

- The strength of your third-party case
- The amount of workers' comp benefits paid
- Whether you reached maximum medical improvement
- Your future need for medical care

## The Real Impact on Your Settlement: Working the Numbers

### Typical Settlement Breakdown

Let's look at a realistic example of how liens affect a $100,000 settlement:

**Gross Settlement:** $100,000

**Deductions:**

- Attorney fees (33%): $33,000
- Case expenses (filing fees, expert witnesses, medical records): $5,000
- Hospital lien (negotiated down from $25,000): $15,000
- Health insurance subrogation (reduced by attorney fee sharing): $8,000
- Medicare lien (with pro-rata reduction): $12,000

**Your Net Recovery:** $27,000

**The Reality Check:** From a $100,000 settlement, you might only receive $27,000 after all liens and fees.

## Why Early Lien Management Matters

**Scenario 1: No Lien Management**

- Liens total $45,000
- No negotiations attempted
- Net recovery: $17,000

**Scenario 2: Aggressive Lien Management**

- Same liens negotiated down to $25,000
- Savings: $20,000
- Net recovery: $37,000

**The Difference:** Proper lien management more than doubled the client's recovery.

## Negotiation Strategies That Actually Work

### For Medical Provider Liens

**The Hardship Approach:** "My client suffered severe injuries and faces ongoing financial difficulties. The settlement barely covers future medical needs. We respectfully request a reduction to help ensure some recovery reaches the injured party."

**The Common Fund Doctrine:** "Your recovery was made possible by our attorney's efforts. Fairness dictates that you should contribute to the legal costs that benefited you."

**The Proportionate Recovery Argument:** "This settlement represents only 40% of the case's full value due to the defendant's limited insurance. Your lien should be reduced proportionally."

**The Itemized Challenge:** "We've identified several charges that don't relate to the accident injuries. We request documentation for these specific items..."

## For Insurance Subrogation

**Attorney Fee Sharing Language:** "Industry standard recognizes that subrogated parties should share in the attorney fees that made their recovery possible. We propose a 33% reduction reflecting the standard contingency fee."

**Proportionate Recovery Calculation:** "The settlement represents [X%] of full damages. Your subrogation should be limited to the same percentage of your claim."

**Settlement vs. Policy Limits Analysis:** "Our client recovered only the defendant's policy limits, which were insufficient to fully compensate the damages. This constitutes a compromise settlement warranting proportionate reduction."

## For Government Liens (Medicare/Medicaid)

**Pro-rata Reduction Request:** "Attorney fees and costs totaled $X. Medicare should bear its proportionate share of these expenses that made recovery possible."

**Hardship Waiver Application:** "Our client faces significant ongoing medical expenses and limited income. We request consideration under the hardship waiver provisions."

**Compromise Settlement Documentation:** "This settlement represents a compromise due to disputed liability and limited insurance coverage, warranting reduction under applicable guidelines."

# Step-by-Step Lien Resolution Process

## Phase 1: Discovery and Documentation (Settlement Day to 30 Days)

**Week 1-2: Lien Identification**

- Request lien notices from all potential claimants
- Review medical records for treatment providers
- Check with insurance companies for subrogation claims
- Search court records for filed liens

**Week 3-4: Verification and Analysis**

- Obtain itemized statements from all lienholders
- Cross-reference charges with medical records
- Identify any duplicate, excessive, or unrelated charges
- Calculate preliminary negotiation targets

## Phase 2: Initial Negotiations (30-60 Days)

**Strategy Development:**

- Prioritize liens by size and negotiation potential
- Prepare standardized reduction request letters
- Gather supporting documentation (financial hardship, case value analysis, etc.)
- Set realistic reduction targets for each lien

**First Round Communications:**

- Send formal lien reduction requests

- Include case-specific arguments for reduction
- Request detailed breakdowns of claimed amounts
- Establish contact with decision-makers

### Phase 3: Aggressive Negotiation (60-90 Days)

**Follow-up Strategy:**

- Phone negotiations with lien representatives
- Present alternative settlement proposals
- Challenge questionable charges
- Leverage multiple lien reductions as package deals

**Documentation Requirements:**

- Get all agreements in writing
- Require lien satisfaction letters
- Confirm final payment amounts
- Establish payment deadlines

### Phase 4: Final Resolution (90-120 Days)

**Payment Processing:**

- Distribute funds according to negotiated agreements
- Obtain lien releases and satisfaction documents
- Provide detailed accounting to client
- Retain documentation for future reference

## Advanced Negotiation Tactics

### The Package Deal Approach

When facing multiple liens, propose reducing all of them together:

"We have $35,000 available for lien resolution. Rather than lengthy individual negotiations, we propose the following package settlement that provides immediate payment to all parties..."

### The Litigation Threat Strategy

For unreasonable lienholders:

"If we cannot reach an amicable resolution, we will be forced to challenge this lien in court, which will delay payment and increase costs for all parties."

### The Future Business Argument

For medical providers:

"Dr. Smith provided excellent care and we hope to refer future clients. A reasonable lien resolution would demonstrate the practice's commitment to patient welfare."

### The Cash Flow Incentive

"We can provide immediate payment upon agreement versus the uncertainty and delay of full collection efforts."

## Sample Lien Reduction Letters

### Medical Provider Lien Reduction Request

[Date]
[Medical Provider Billing Department]
[Address]

RE: Lien Reduction Request - [Patient Name] / DOB: [Date] / Account: [Number]

Dear Billing Manager,

I represent [Client Name] in connection with injuries sustained in an accident on [Date]. Your facility provided excellent medical care totaling $[Amount], for which a lien has been filed.

Due to the circumstances of this case, I respectfully request a reduction of your lien to $[Proposed Amount] for the following reasons:

1. **Limited Settlement Recovery:** The total settlement of $[Amount] represents only [X%] of the case's full value due to the defendant's inadequate insurance coverage.

2. **Significant Legal Expenses:** Attorney fees and costs totaled $[Amount], leaving limited funds for lien resolution.

3. **Ongoing Financial Hardship:** My client faces continued medical expenses and lost income, making full payment extremely difficult.

4. **Prompt Payment Benefit:** This proposal provides immediate payment versus uncertain collection prospects.

I have enclosed a detailed breakdown of the settlement distribution and supporting documentation. Your consideration of this request would be greatly appreciated and would allow for prompt resolution.

I look forward to your response within 30 days.

Sincerely,
[Attorney Name]
[Contact Information]

## Health Insurance Subrogation Reduction Request

[Date]

[Insurance Company Subrogation Department]
[Address]

RE: Subrogation Claim Reduction - Policy #[Number] / Claim #[Number]

Dear Subrogation Representative,

I represent [Insured Name] regarding the third-party recovery for injuries sustained on [Date]. Your company paid medical benefits totaling $[Amount] and has asserted a subrogation claim for full reimbursement.

I respectfully request a reduction of your subrogation claim to $[Proposed Amount] based on the following legal principles:

1. **Common Fund Doctrine:** Your recovery was made possible through the efforts and expenses of our legal representation. Equity requires sharing in these costs.

2. **Proportionate Recovery:** The settlement of $[Amount] represents only [X%] of full damages due to [defendant's limited insurance/disputed liability]. Your subrogation should be reduced proportionally.

3. **Attorney Fee Sharing:** Industry standard recognizes that subrogated parties should contribute to attorney fees. A [X%] reduction reflects this principle.

The enclosed settlement breakdown demonstrates that this compromise serves the interests of all parties while ensuring some recovery reaches your insured. I would welcome the opportunity to discuss this matter further and reach a mutually acceptable resolution.

Sincerely,

[Attorney Name]
[Contact Information]

## Government Lien Procedures

### Medicare Lien Resolution Process

**Step 1: Obtain Conditional Payment Summary**

- Contact Medicare's Benefits Coordination & Recovery Center (BCRC)
- Request all payments related to the injury
- Review for accuracy and completeness

**Step 2: Report Settlement**

- Use Medicare's online portal or submit required forms
- Include settlement amount and date
- Provide attorney and case information

**Step 3: Request Final Demand**

- Submit request with settlement documentation

- Include attorney fee and cost breakdown
- Wait for Medicare's final calculation

**Step 4: Negotiate Reduction**

- Challenge any unrelated medical payments
- Request pro-rata reduction for attorney fees/costs
- Apply for hardship waiver if applicable

**Step 5: Final Payment**

- Pay agreed amount within 120 days
- Obtain satisfaction letter
- Retain documentation

## Medicaid Lien Resolution

**State Notification Requirements:**

- Contact your state's Medicaid recovery unit
- Provide case information and settlement details
- Request itemized list of payments

**Ahlborn Allocation Strategy:**

- Prepare detailed settlement breakdown
- Allocate damages between medical expenses and other categories
- Limit Medicaid recovery to medical expense portion only

**Documentation Package:**

- Settlement agreement with damage breakdown
- Medical records and bills
- Expert testimony on damage allocation
- Comparative case law

## Common Lien Mistakes to Avoid

### Mistake #1: Ignoring Lien Notices

**The Problem:** Hoping liens will go away or assuming they're invalid **The Consequence:** Interest, penalties, and collection actions **The Solution:** Address every lien notice promptly and professionally

### Mistake #2: Accepting the First Demand

**The Problem:** Paying liens at face value without negotiation **The Consequence:** Leaving thousands of dollars on the table **The Solution:** Always request itemized statements and negotiate reductions

### Mistake #3: Poor Record Keeping

**The Problem:** Losing track of lien communications and agreements **The Consequence:** Disputes over payment amounts and terms **The Solution:** Maintain detailed files with all lien-related documents

### Mistake #4: Mixing Injury-Related and Non-Related Medical Bills

**The Problem:** Allowing lienholders to claim payment for unrelated medical care **The Consequence:** Inflated lien amounts **The Solution:** Carefully review all claimed expenses for relevance to the injury

### Mistake #5: Missing Government Lien Deadlines

**The Problem:** Failing to report settlements or pay liens within required timeframes **The Consequence:** Penalties, interest, and potential legal action **The Solution:** Create timeline tracking systems for all government lien requirements

## Special Situations and Advanced Strategies

### Structured Settlements and Liens

When considering a structured settlement, liens can complicate the analysis:

**Immediate Lien Payment Requirement:** Most liens must be paid from the initial lump sum, reducing the amount available for structuring.

**Future Payment Protection:** Properly resolved liens cannot attach to future structured settlement payments.

**Tax Considerations:** Lien payments may affect the tax treatment of settlement proceeds.

### Multiple Defendant Cases

When several parties share fault, lien resolution becomes more complex:

**Joint and Several Liability:** Lienholders may claim against any defendant's payment.

**Proportionate Share Arguments:** Argue that liens should be reduced based on your defendant's percentage of fault.

**Settlement Timing:** Coordinate lien negotiations with multiple settlement discussions.

### Bankruptcy and Liens

Personal injury settlements receive special treatment in bankruptcy:

**Exemption Planning:** Some settlement proceeds may be protected from creditors.

**Lien Survival:** Most injury-related liens survive bankruptcy discharge.

**Timing Strategies:** Consider bankruptcy timing in relation to settlement and lien resolution.

## Technology and Lien Management

### Digital Tools for Lien Tracking

**Spreadsheet Templates:**

- Lien amount and contact information
- Negotiation history and outcomes

- Payment deadlines and requirements
- Document storage locations

**Case Management Software:**

- Automated deadline tracking
- Document management systems
- Communication logs
- Financial accounting integration

**Online Resources:**

- Medicare BCRC portal
- State Medicaid recovery websites
- Insurance company subrogation departments
- Medical provider billing systems

# Working with Your Attorney on Lien Issues

## Questions to Ask Your Attorney

1. "What liens do you expect in my case?"
2. "What's your strategy for reducing each lien?"
3. "How will lien negotiations affect my settlement timeline?"
4. "What's the worst-case scenario for lien amounts?"
5. "Can you provide regular updates on lien negotiations?"

## Red Flags in Attorney Lien Management

- Waiting until after settlement to address liens
- Failing to negotiate any lien reductions
- Not providing detailed accounting of lien payments

- Rushing to settle without lien verification
- Inadequate documentation of lien agreements

### When to Consider Lien-Specific Counsel

Some cases may benefit from attorneys who specialize in lien resolution:

- Complex Medicare/Medicaid liens
- Multiple ERISA plan claims
- High-value cases with numerous liens
- Disputed lien validity issues
- Government enforcement actions

## The Future of Lien Management

### Emerging Trends

**Increased Automation:** Insurance companies and government agencies are using automated systems to identify and pursue subrogation claims more aggressively.

**Data Mining:** Advanced data analysis helps lienholders identify settlement cases more efficiently.

**Standardized Procedures:** Many organizations are adopting uniform lien resolution procedures to streamline negotiations.

**Alternative Dispute Resolution:** Some lienholders now offer mediation or arbitration for disputed claims.

### Legislative Changes

**State Law Variations:** States continue to modify their lien and subrogation laws, sometimes favoring injured parties.

**Federal Updates:** Medicare and Medicaid procedures are regularly updated, requiring ongoing attention to compliance requirements.

**Insurance Reform:** Some states are considering legislation to limit subrogation claims or require attorney fee sharing.

## Final Checklist: Maximizing Your Settlement Recovery

### Before Settlement

- [ ] Identify all potential lienholders
- [ ] Obtain itemized statements from medical providers
- [ ] Review insurance policies for subrogation clauses
- [ ] Check for government benefit payments
- [ ] Organize all medical records and bills
- [ ] Document any unrelated medical expenses

### During Negotiations

- [ ] Challenge questionable charges
- [ ] Request lien reductions from all parties
- [ ] Use leverage from multiple lien negotiations
- [ ] Document all agreements in writing
- [ ] Confirm final payment amounts
- [ ] Establish payment deadlines

### After Settlement

- [ ] Verify lien payments are made correctly
- [ ] Obtain satisfaction letters from all lienholders
- [ ] Retain all documentation
- [ ] Monitor for any post-settlement collection attempts
- [ ] Confirm compliance with government reporting requirements

## Key Takeaways

**Most Important Points:**

1. **Nearly every lien can be negotiated** - Don't accept the first demand
2. **Early intervention saves money** - Address liens before settlement when possible
3. **Documentation is crucial** - Keep detailed records of all lien-related communications
4. **Government liens require special attention** - Medicare and Medicaid have strict compliance requirements
5. **Professional help pays for itself** - Experienced attorneys can often negotiate significant lien reductions

**Your Action Plan:**

1. Work with your attorney to identify all potential liens early in your case
2. Maintain organized records of all medical treatment and communications
3. Don't be afraid to negotiate - most lienholders expect to reduce their claims
4. Get all agreements in writing before making any payments
5. Keep detailed records for future reference and protection

**Remember:** Proper lien management can often increase your settlement recovery by 25-50% or more. The time and effort invested in this process typically pays substantial dividends in your final recovery amount.

*This guide provides general information about settlement liens and should not be considered legal advice for specific situations. Always consult with qualified legal counsel for guidance on your particular case.*

23

# Tax Implications of Personal Injury Settlements

*What Part of Your Settlement is Tax-Free*

One of the most common questions personal injury clients ask is whether they'll owe taxes on their settlement or court award. The uncertainty is understandable - after dealing with injuries, medical bills, and legal proceedings, the last thing you want is an unexpected tax bill. The good news is that most personal injury compensation is tax-free, but there are important exceptions you need to understand.

## The General Rule: Your Settlement Is Probably Tax-Free

Under federal tax law (specifically Section 104(a)(2) of the Internal Revenue Code), compensation you receive for physical injuries is generally not considered taxable income. This tax exemption covers the core elements of most personal injury settlements:

**Medical expenses** - Whether past, present, or future medical costs, reimbursement for treatment related to your physical injury is not taxable.

**Pain and suffering** - Compensation for the physical pain and emotional distress directly resulting from your physical injury remains tax-free.

**Lost wages** - Money awarded to replace income you lost due to time off work for your physical injury is not taxable when received as part of a personal injury settlement.

**Disability-related damages** - Compensation for permanent physical impairment or loss of function is exempt from taxation.

The key phrase here is "physical injury." The tax code draws a clear distinction between compensation for physical harm and other types of damages, which leads us to the important exceptions.

## When You Will Owe Taxes: The Key Exceptions

While most personal injury settlements are tax-free, certain components are always taxable, regardless of the nature of your underlying injury:

### Punitive Damages Are Always Taxable

Punitive damages - money awarded to punish the defendant rather than compensate you for losses - are fully taxable as ordinary income. This is true even if they're part of a settlement for severe physical injuries. You must report punitive damages as "Other Income" on your tax return, and you'll owe income tax at your regular tax rate.

**Example**: If you receive $100,000 for medical expenses and pain and suffering (tax-free) plus $25,000 in punitive damages, you'll owe income tax on the $25,000 punitive award.

### Interest on Court Judgments

If your case goes to trial and you're awarded interest (such as post-judgment interest that accrues while waiting for payment), that interest portion is taxable income. The underlying award remains tax-free, but interest is treated like any other investment income.

### Emotional Distress Without Physical Injury

This is where the tax rules become more complex. If your case involves emotional distress or mental anguish that stems directly from a physical injury, that compensation remains tax-free. However, if you're compensated for emotional harm without any corresponding physical injury - such as in harassment, defamation, or employment discrimination cases - the award may be taxable.

**The physical injury requirement**: Courts and the IRS look for actual physical injuries, not just physical manifestations of emotional distress. Headaches, insomnia, or stomach problems caused by emotional trauma typically don't qualify as "physical injury" for tax purposes.

### Previously Deducted Medical Expenses

If you itemized deductions on past tax returns and claimed medical expenses related to your accident, and those same expenses are later reimbursed through your settlement, you may need to include the reimbursement as taxable income. This prevents you from getting a "double benefit" - both a tax deduction and tax-free reimbursement for the same expenses.

## How Settlement Allocation Affects Your Taxes

When your settlement involves multiple types of damages, proper allocation becomes crucial for tax purposes. Your attorney should work with you to clearly specify in the settlement agreement how much money is allocated to each category:

- Medical expenses and related costs
- Pain and suffering from physical injury
- Lost wages due to physical injury
- Punitive damages
- Emotional distress (with or without physical injury)
- Pre-judgment or post-judgment interest

Clear allocation serves several purposes: it documents which portions are tax-free, helps you report any taxable income accurately, and can be valuable if the IRS ever questions your tax filing.

## Understanding IRS Form 1099

Depending on your settlement structure, you may or may not receive tax forms:

**When you'll get a 1099**: If any portion of your settlement is taxable (like punitive damages), the insurance company or defendant may send you Form 1099-MISC reporting the taxable amount.

**When you won't get a 1099**: Pure personal injury settlements for physical injuries typically don't trigger a 1099 because they're not taxable income.

**Important**: Even if you don't receive a 1099, you're still responsible for accurately reporting any taxable portions of your settlement. The absence of a form doesn't make taxable income non-taxable.

## State Tax Considerations

**New York**: Generally follows federal tax rules for personal injury settlements. Tax-free settlements under federal law are typically tax-free for New York state purposes as well.

**California**: Also mirrors federal guidelines, treating most personal injury compensation as non-taxable. However, California has its own tax code nuances, so consulting with a tax professional familiar with California law is advisable for larger settlements.

**Other states**: Most states follow federal tax treatment for personal injury awards, but some have unique provisions. Always verify the rules in your state, especially if you live in a state with high income tax rates.

## When to Consult a Tax Professional

Consider working with a certified public accountant (CPA) or tax attorney if:

- Your settlement includes punitive damages or other potentially taxable components
- You previously claimed tax deductions for medical expenses related to your injury
- Your settlement is structured to provide payments over multiple

years

- You're unsure about the tax treatment of any part of your award
- You have questions about estimated tax payments if you owe taxes on the settlement
- Your case involves complex allocation issues between taxable and non-taxable damages

Many personal injury attorneys work closely with tax professionals to help clients structure settlements in the most tax-efficient manner possible.

## Practical Steps to Protect Yourself

**Document everything**: Keep detailed records of your settlement agreement, especially how damages are allocated between different categories.

**Plan for tax payments**: If your settlement includes taxable components, set aside money for taxes immediately. Don't spend money you'll owe to the IRS.

**Consider timing**: If you have control over when you receive taxable portions of your settlement, consider the timing in relation to your other income and tax situation.

**Get professional help early**: Tax planning is most effective before you finalize your settlement, not after you've already received the money.

## The Bottom Line

The majority of personal injury settlements - those compensating you for medical expenses, pain and suffering, and lost wages related to physical injuries - are completely tax-free. This tax exemption recognizes that you're being made whole for losses and harm you've suffered, not receiving windfall income.

However, punitive damages, interest, and certain types of emotional distress awards are taxable, and proper planning can help you minimize any tax burden. Understanding these distinctions and working with qualified professionals ensures you can focus on your recovery without worrying about unexpected tax consequences.

The tax implications of your settlement are just one piece of moving forward after a personal injury case. In our next discussion, we'll explore the broader picture of life after settlement - how to manage your compensation wisely, protect your financial future, and focus on healing and recovery.

# 24

# Moving Forward After the Claim

*Starting Fresh After Your Case Ends*

Resolving a personal injury claim represents a significant milestone in your journey, but it's important to understand that reaching a settlement or completing a trial doesn't mark the end of your story. The phase that follows is equally crucial, as it involves rebuilding your life, managing any long-term impacts from your injury, and navigating potential legal and financial challenges that may arise. This comprehensive guide will help you move forward confidently in the physical, emotional, and legal aspects of your post-claim life.

## Understanding and Managing Long-Term Injuries

Many personal injuries leave lasting effects that extend far beyond the resolution of your legal case. Chronic pain conditions, reduced mobility, cognitive changes, or psychological trauma may persist long after you've received your settlement or court award. Recognizing and addressing these ongoing challenges is essential for your long-term well-being.

**Continuing Your Medical Care**

Your relationship with your healthcare providers shouldn't end when your legal case concludes. Continue following all treatment recommendations from your medical team, including physical therapy, occupational therapy, pain management, or specialized care. Regular follow-up appointments help monitor your condition and can catch potential complications early. If you're experiencing new symptoms or your condition appears to be worsening, don't hesitate to seek additional medical evaluation.

**Building Your Support Network**

Recovery often involves more than medical treatment alone. Consider joining support groups for individuals who have experienced similar injuries or trauma. These groups provide valuable emotional support, practical advice, and the opportunity to connect with others who truly understand your experience. Many hospitals, community centers, and online platforms offer such resources.

Mental health support is equally important. Speaking with a counselor, therapist, or psychologist can help you process the emotional impact of your injury and develop healthy coping strategies. Many people find that addressing the psychological aspects of their injury is just as important as treating the physical symptoms.

**Workplace and Career Considerations**

If your injury affects your ability to perform your job duties, explore options for workplace accommodations under the Americans with Disabilities Act. These might include modified work schedules, ergonomic equipment, or adjusted responsibilities. If returning to your previous role isn't possible, consider vocational rehabilitation services or job retraining programs that can help you transition to new employment opportunities that better suit your current capabilities.

Staying proactive in your recovery efforts not only supports your healing process but also helps preserve your legal rights should your condition unexpectedly worsen or new complications arise in the future.

## Strategic Financial Planning and Recovery

Receiving a settlement or court award, whether as a lump sum or structured payments, presents both significant opportunities and potential risks. Proper financial planning is crucial for ensuring your settlement provides long-term security rather than short-term relief.

### Professional Financial Guidance

Consider consulting with a financial planner who has specific experience in personal injury settlements and understands the unique challenges injury victims face. These professionals can help you create a comprehensive financial strategy that accounts for your ongoing medical needs, potential future care costs, and long-term financial goals.

### Budgeting for Your New Reality

Create a detailed budget that reflects your current situation, including ongoing medical expenses, therapy costs, medication expenses, and any modifications needed for your home or vehicle. Factor in potential changes to your earning capacity and plan for inflation in medical costs over time. Remember that some medical needs may increase as you age or if your condition progresses.

### Tax Considerations

While most personal injury settlements are not taxable, certain portions may be subject to taxation, particularly punitive damages or interest earned on delayed payments. Consult with a tax professional to understand your specific obligations and consider setting aside funds to cover any potential tax liabilities.

### Asset Protection Strategies

Protect your settlement from potential creditors or poor financial decisions by exploring options such as structured settlements, annuities, or trust arrangements. These vehicles can provide steady income over time while protecting your principal from market volatility or impulsive spending decisions.

### Special Circumstances

For settlements involving minors or individuals with disabilities, special legal structures may be necessary. Special needs trusts can preserve eligibility for government benefits like Medicaid or Supplemental Security Income while still providing access to settlement funds for approved expenses. Guardianship or conservatorship arrangements may also be appropriate in certain situations.

## Rebuilding Your Credit and Employment Status

Personal injuries often create financial disruption that can damage your credit score and employment history. Taking proactive steps to address these issues is essential for your long-term financial health.

**Credit Restoration**

Begin by obtaining copies of your credit reports from all three major credit bureaus. Review them carefully for accuracy and dispute any errors you find. If your injury led to missed payments or unpaid medical bills, contact your creditors to explain your situation and negotiate payment plans or settlements. Many creditors are willing to work with injury victims, especially when you can demonstrate a clear plan for repayment.

Consider working with a certified nonprofit credit counseling agency, which can help you develop a debt management plan and provide education on rebuilding your credit over time. Be cautious of for-profit credit repair companies that may charge high fees for services you can often perform yourself.

**Employment Recovery**

If your injury affected your employment status or earning capacity, explore available resources for getting back into the workforce. Vocational rehabilitation services can help you identify new career paths that accommodate any permanent limitations from your injury. Many state agencies offer these services at no cost to qualified individuals.

If you face discrimination in employment due to your injury or disability, consider consulting with an employment attorney or contacting the Equal Employment Opportunity Commission. Federal and state laws provide protections for individuals with disabilities, and you have the right to reasonable accommodations in the workplace.

## Ongoing Legal Considerations

Even after your personal injury case concludes, several legal issues may require attention in the future.

**Future Medical Complications**

If you develop new symptoms or complications that may be related to your original injury, consult with your attorney about whether you have grounds for additional legal action. This is particularly relevant in cases involving medical malpractice, defective products, or toxic exposures where health effects may not manifest for years.

Keep in mind that most settlements include releases that prevent future claims against the same defendant for the same incident. However, if new defendants are identified or entirely separate incidents occur, you may still have legal recourse.

### Judgment Enforcement

If your case resulted in a court judgment rather than a settlement, the losing party is legally obligated to pay the awarded amount. However, collecting on judgments can sometimes be challenging. If the defendant fails to pay as ordered, your attorney may need to take additional legal action to enforce the judgment, which might include wage garnishment, asset seizure, or other collection methods.

### Government Benefits and Reporting Requirements

If you receive government benefits such as Social Security Disability, Medicare, or Medicaid, you may be required to report your settlement to these agencies. Failure to report could result in benefit termination or demands for repayment of previously received benefits. Work with your attorney or a benefits specialist to ensure compliance with all reporting requirements.

### Document Preservation

Maintain organized files containing all legal documents, settlement agreements, medical records, and correspondence related to your case. These documents may be needed in the future for tax purposes, benefit applications, or if new legal issues arise. Consider keeping both physical and digital copies in secure locations.

## Personal Reflection and Moving Forward

The process of pursuing a personal injury claim is emotionally and physically demanding. As you transition to the next phase of your life, take time to acknowledge what you've endured and recognize your strength in navigating this challenging experience.

### Finding Meaning and Purpose

Many injury survivors find it empowering to channel their experience into helping others. Consider volunteering for organizations focused on injury prevention, safety advocacy, or supporting other injury victims. Sharing your story, when you're ready and comfortable doing so, can raise awareness about important safety issues and provide hope to others facing similar challenges.

**Pursuing New Interests and Activities**

Your injury may have changed your physical capabilities, but it doesn't define your potential for finding joy and fulfillment in life. Explore new hobbies, creative outlets, or physical activities that work within your current limitations. Many people discover hidden talents or interests they never would have explored otherwise.

**Building Resilience**

Recovery is not just about returning to your previous state but about building resilience and adapting to your new circumstances. This might involve developing new coping strategies, strengthening relationships, or discovering inner resources you didn't know you possessed.

## Your Path Forward

Life after a personal injury claim involves multiple dimensions of recovery - emotional, physical, and financial. While the legal process has concluded, your journey of healing and rebuilding continues. The key to success lies in staying informed about your options, remaining proactive in addressing challenges, and not hesitating to seek professional help when needed.

Remember that recovery is not a linear process, and there will likely be both good days and difficult ones ahead. Be patient with yourself and celebrate small victories along the way. With proper planning, appropriate support, and a commitment to your well-being, you can regain control of your future and move forward with confidence.

Your experience, while undoubtedly difficult, has also demonstrated your resilience and determination. These qualities will serve you well as you write the next chapters of your life story. The injury you sustained does not define who you are, but how you choose to respond to it can profoundly shape your future.

Thank you for taking the time to read this guide. May it serve as a trusted resource as you continue to advocate for yourself, protect your rights, and work toward rebuilding and reclaiming your life. Your journey continues, and with the right knowledge and support, your best days can still lie ahead.

# Glossary of Legal Terms

## *Legal Words Made Easy to Understand*

---

### A

**Actual Cause** - Also known as "cause in fact"; the direct cause of an injury where the harm would not have occurred but for the defendant's actions.

**Adjuster** - An insurance company representative who investigates claims and determines settlement amounts on behalf of the insurer.

**Alternative Dispute Resolution (ADR)** - Methods of resolving disputes outside of traditional litigation, including mediation and arbitration.

**Arbitration** - A formal dispute resolution process where a neutral arbitrator makes a binding or non-binding decision after hearing evidence from both parties.

**Assault** - An intentional tort involving the threat or attempt to cause harmful or offensive contact with another person.

**Assumption of Risk** - A legal defense claiming the plaintiff voluntarily exposed themselves to a known danger and should bear responsibility for resulting harm.

# B

**Battery** - An intentional tort involving harmful or offensive physical contact with another person without their consent.

**Bench Trial** - A trial decided by a judge rather than a jury.

**Breach of Duty** - The failure to meet the standard of care owed to another person, forming one of the four elements of negligence.

**Burden of Proof** - The obligation to prove one's case. In civil cases, typically requires "preponderance of the evidence."

# C

**Causation** - The connection between a defendant's breach of duty and the plaintiff's injury, including both actual cause and proximate cause.

**Comparative Negligence** - A legal doctrine that reduces a plaintiff's compensation based on their percentage of fault in causing the incident.

**Complaint** - The initial legal document filed to start a lawsuit, outlining the facts and legal claims.

**Contingency Fee** - A payment arrangement where an attorney receives a percentage of the recovery (typically 33-40%) only if the case is successful.

**Contributory Negligence** - A harsh legal doctrine (not used in NY or CA) that completely bars recovery if the plaintiff contributed to their own injury.

# D

**Damages** - Monetary compensation awarded to a plaintiff, including:

- *Economic Damages*: Measurable financial losses (medical bills, lost wages)
- *Non-Economic Damages*: Intangible losses (pain and suffering)
- *Punitive Damages*: Awards meant to punish egregious conduct

**Defendant** - The party being sued or accused of wrongdoing in a lawsuit.

**Deposition** - Sworn out-of-court testimony taken during the discovery phase, typically conducted in an attorney's office with a court reporter present.

**Discovery** - The pre-trial phase where both parties exchange information and evidence relevant to the case through various tools like depositions, interrogatories, and document requests.

**Discovery Rule** - A legal principle that starts the statute of limitations when an injury is discovered rather than when it occurred, often applied in medical malpractice cases.

**Duty of Care** - A legal obligation requiring individuals to exercise reasonable care to prevent harm to others.

## E

**Economic Damages** - Tangible, measurable financial losses resulting from an injury, such as medical expenses and lost wages.

**ERISA** - Employee Retirement Income Security Act; federal law governing employer-sponsored benefit plans that often contain subrogation rights.

**Expert Witness** - A person with specialized knowledge permitted to testify about technical matters within their area of expertise.

## F

**False Imprisonment** - An intentional tort involving the unlawful restraint of a person's freedom of movement.

**First-Party Claim** - An insurance claim filed with your own insurance company.

## G

**Government Claim** - A special type of claim against public entities that typically requires shorter filing deadlines and specific notice procedures.

## I

**IME (Independent Medical Examination)** - A medical evaluation performed by a doctor chosen by the defense to assess the plaintiff's injury claims.

**Intentional Infliction of Emotional Distress** - A tort involving extreme and outrageous conduct intended to cause severe emotional distress.

**Intentional Tort** - A wrongful act done deliberately that causes harm (examples: assault, battery, defamation).

**Interrogatories** - Written questions sent by one party to another during discovery that must be answered under oath.

## J

**Judgment** - The final decision of a court in a lawsuit.

**Jury Trial** - A trial where a jury of peers decides the facts and verdict.

## L

**Liability** - Legal responsibility for one's actions or omissions that cause harm to another.

**Lien** - A legal right to a portion of a settlement or judgment held by a third party (such as a medical provider or insurance company) who provided benefits related to the injury.

**Litigation** - The process of resolving disputes through the court system.

**Loss of Consortium** - Damages awarded for the negative impact an injury has on a spouse's relationship, including companionship and intimacy.

## M

**Medical Malpractice** - Professional negligence by healthcare providers that results in patient harm.

**Mediation** - A voluntary dispute resolution process where a neutral mediator helps parties explore settlement options.

**Motion** - A formal request to the court for a specific ruling or order.

**Multiplier Method** - A common way to calculate non-economic damages by multiplying economic damages by a factor (typically 1.5 to 5) based on injury severity.

# N

**Negligence** - The failure to exercise reasonable care that a prudent person would use under similar circumstances, resulting in harm to another.

**No-Fault Insurance** - An insurance system (used in New York) where each party's own insurance covers their losses regardless of who caused the accident.

**Non-Economic Damages** - Compensation for intangible losses such as pain and suffering, emotional distress, and loss of enjoyment of life.

**Notice of Claim** - A formal notice required to be filed against government entities within strict time limits (typically 90 days in NY, 6 months in CA).

# P

**Pain and Suffering** - Non-economic damages compensating for physical pain and emotional distress resulting from an injury.

**Personal Injury Protection (PIP)** - No-fault insurance coverage that pays for medical expenses and other benefits regardless of fault (mandatory in New York).

**Plaintiff** - The person who initiates a lawsuit seeking compensation for harm.

**Premises Liability** - Legal responsibility of property owners to maintain safe conditions for visitors.

**Preponderance of the Evidence** - The standard of proof in civil cases; requires showing that a claim is more likely true than not (greater than 50% probability).

**Product Liability** - Legal responsibility of manufacturers and sellers for injuries caused by defective products.

**Proximate Cause** - A cause that is legally sufficient to result in liability; the injury must be a foreseeable result of the defendant's actions.

**Punitive Damages** - Monetary awards designed to punish defendants for particularly egregious conduct and deter similar behavior.

# R

**Release** - A legal document that settles a claim and prevents future lawsuits related to the same incident.

**Request for Production** - A discovery tool used to obtain documents, records, or physical evidence from the opposing party.

# S

**Settlement** - A legally binding agreement resolving a claim without going to trial.

**Serious Injury** - Under New York's no-fault law, injuries that meet specific thresholds allowing victims to sue for pain and suffering (includes fractures, significant disfigurement, permanent limitations).

**Statute of Limitations** - The legal deadline by which a lawsuit must be filed (3 years in NY, 2 years in CA for most personal injury cases).

**Strict Liability** - Legal responsibility imposed regardless of fault or negligence, commonly applied to defective products and certain animal injuries.

**Structured Settlement** - A settlement paid in installments over time rather than as a lump sum.

**Subrogation** - The right of an insurance company to seek reimbursement from a settlement or judgment for benefits they paid on behalf of the injured party.

# T

**Third-Party Claim** - An insurance claim filed against the insurance company of the party responsible for the injury.

**Tort** - A civil wrong (other than breach of contract) that causes harm and provides grounds for a lawsuit.

**Trial** - A formal court proceeding where evidence is presented and a judge or jury decides the outcome.

# U

**Uninsured/Underinsured Motorist Coverage (UM/UIM)** - Insurance protection for accidents caused by drivers with no insurance or insufficient coverage.

# V

**Verdict** - The decision reached by a jury or judge at the end of a trial.

**Voir Dire** - The jury selection process where potential jurors are questioned to assess their suitability and impartiality.

# W

**Workers' Compensation** - A system providing benefits to employees injured on the job, typically barring lawsuits against employers.

**Wrongful Death** - A legal claim brought when a person dies as a result of another's wrongful act or negligence.

*This glossary provides essential terminology for understanding personal injury law in New York and California. For specific legal advice, always consult with a qualified attorney in your jurisdiction.*

# Motor Vehicle Accident Emergency Checklist

## *Quick Steps to Take After a Crash*

---

### Immediate Actions at the Scene

**1. Ensure Safety First**

- Move your vehicle to a safe location if possible (shoulder, parking lot)
- Turn on hazard lights immediately
- Set up flares or reflective triangles if available
- If vehicles cannot be moved safely, leave them where they are
- Call 911 immediately for any injuries, significant damage, or if the accident blocks traffic
- Even if injuries seem minor, consider calling for medical assistance

**2. Exchange Essential Information** Collect the following from ALL parties involved:

- Full legal names of drivers and passengers
- Phone numbers and addresses
- Driver's license numbers
- Insurance company names and policy numbers
- Vehicle information: make, model, year, color, VIN, and license plate numbers
- Location of the accident (exact address or nearest intersection)

**3. Document Everything Thoroughly** Take photos of:

- The overall accident scene from multiple angles
- All vehicle damage (close-up and wide shots)
- License plates of all vehicles
- The other driver's insurance card and driver's license
- Street signs, traffic signals, and road conditions
- Any visible injuries
- Skid marks, debris, or other evidence
- Weather and lighting conditions

**4. Gather Witness Information**

- Collect names and phone numbers of any witnesses
- Ask witnesses to provide a brief written statement if possible
- Get their email addresses for follow-up contact
- Note their location during the accident

## Critical Communication Guidelines

**5. Protect Yourself Legally**

- DO NOT admit fault or say "I'm sorry" - these statements can be used against you

- Stick to factual observations only: "I was traveling north on Main Street"
- Avoid discussing details of how the accident happened with other parties
- Be polite but limit conversation to necessary information exchange
- If the other party becomes aggressive, stay in your vehicle and wait for police

**6. Work with Law Enforcement**

- Provide honest, factual information to responding officers
- Request the police report number and ask how to obtain a copy
- Get the responding officer's name and badge number
- If police don't respond, file an accident report at the nearest police station

## Post-Accident Medical and Legal Priorities

**7. Seek Medical Attention Immediately**

- Get medical evaluation even if you feel fine - adrenaline can mask injuries
- Some injuries (whiplash, concussion, soft tissue damage) may not show symptoms for hours or days
- Keep all medical records, bills, and documentation
- Follow through with all recommended treatment and appointments
- If you decline medical attention at the scene, see your doctor within 24-48 hours

**8. Contact Your Insurance Company**

- Report the accident as soon as possible (within 24 hours is ideal)
- Provide them with all collected information and photos
- Be honest about what happened

- Ask about rental car coverage and other benefits
- Keep detailed records of all conversations, including dates, times, and representative names

## Long-Term Documentation and Recovery

**9. Start a Detailed Recovery Journal** Document daily:

- Physical pain levels and symptoms
- Missed work days and lost wages
- Medical appointments and treatments
- How injuries affect daily activities
- Emotional impacts (anxiety, sleep problems, etc.)
- Out-of-pocket expenses related to the accident

**10. Preserve All Evidence**

- Keep damaged personal items that were in the vehicle
- Save all medical records, bills, and receipts
- Maintain copies of all insurance correspondence
- Store photos and videos in multiple locations (cloud storage, phone, computer)
- Keep a file with all accident-related documents

**11. Know When to Consult an Attorney** Consider legal consultation if:

- You sustained serious injuries requiring ongoing treatment
- Fault for the accident is disputed
- The other party's insurance company denies your claim
- Settlement offers seem insufficient for your damages
- The other driver was uninsured or underinsured
- You're facing significant medical bills or lost wages

## Important Legal Deadlines

**State-Specific Reporting Requirements:**

- **New York:** File DMV accident report within 10 days if injury/death occurred or property damage exceeds $1,000; insurance claims must be filed within 30 days
- **California:** DMV report required within 10 days for injury/death or property damage over $1,000; insurance claim deadlines vary from 30 days to 2 years depending on claim type
- **Check your state's specific requirements** - deadlines vary significantly

## Additional State-Specific Considerations

**No-Fault vs. At-Fault States:**

- No-fault states (like New York): Your insurance pays regardless of who caused the accident
- At-fault states (like California): The responsible party's insurance typically pays
- Understanding your state's system affects how you handle claims and medical bills

## Emergency Contacts Template

*Fill this out and keep with your insurance cards:*

- Insurance Company: ___________________ Phone: ___________________
- Policy Number: ___________________
- Agent Name: ___________________ Phone: ___________________
- Preferred Hospital: ___________________
- Emergency Contact: ___________________ Phone: ___________________

- Attorney (if applicable): __________________ Phone: __________________

**Remember:** This checklist is for general guidance. Laws vary by state, and every accident situation is unique. When in doubt, prioritize safety and seek professional advice from medical providers, insurance representatives, and legal counsel as appropriate.

# Checklist For The Wallet

## *A Pocket-Sized Guide to Protect Yourself*

### AT THE SCENE

☐ **SAFETY FIRST**

- Move to safe area
- Hazards on, call 911

☐ **GET INFO FROM ALL DRIVERS**

- Names & phone numbers
- Insurance company & policy #
- Driver's license #s
- Vehicle: make/model/year/plate

☐ **TAKE PHOTOS**

- Scene from all angles
- All vehicle damage
- License plates

- Other driver's insurance card

□ **WITNESSES**

- Names & phone numbers
- Brief statements if possible

## PROTECT YOURSELF

□ **DO NOT admit fault** □ **Stick to facts only** □ **Get police report number**

## AFTER THE SCENE

□ **SEE DOCTOR** (even if you feel fine) □ **CALL YOUR INSURANCE** (within 24 hrs) □ **START INJURY JOURNAL**

- Daily pain levels
- Missed work
- Medical appointments

□ **SAVE EVERYTHING**

- Medical records & bills
- All photos & documents
- Insurance correspondence

## DEADLINES TO REMEMBER

**NY:** DMV report within 10 days **CA:** DMV report within 10 days **Insurance:** File ASAP (varies by state)

# WHEN TO CALL A LAWYER

- Serious injuries
- Fault is disputed
- Insurance denies claim
- Settlement too low

**EMERGENCY CONTACTS**

Insurance: _________________

Policy #: __________________

Agent: ____________________

Doctor: ___________________

Emergency: ________________

# About the Author

Ngozi E. Bolin, Esq. brings over three decades of extensive litigation experience to this comprehensive guide on personal injury law. With a distinguished career spanning multiple jurisdictions, Ms. Bolin offers readers the benefit of her deep legal knowledge and practical courtroom wisdom.

Educated under the British Commonwealth system and having studied at the Harvard Extension School, Ms. Bolin possesses a uniquely broad legal perspective. Her international credentials began with her admission as a Barrister & Solicitor of the Supreme Court of Nigeria in 1989. She subsequently moved to the United States, gaining admission to the New York State Bar in 1991, the United States Court of Appeals for the Second Circuit, and the California State Bar in 2013.

Throughout her career as a skilled trial attorney, Ms. Bolin has dedicated herself to making legal knowledge accessible and affordable through unbundled services that help consumers understand and assert their rights. Her expertise encompasses a remarkable range of legal disciplines, including personal injury, medical malpractice, legal malpractice, employment law (both individual and class action cases), premises liability, HOA disputes, real estate matters, bankruptcy (Chapters 7 and 11), probate, estate planning, matrimonial law, insurance disputes, appeals, and alternative dispute resolution.

Ms. Bolin has successfully negotiated countless settlements throughout her career, demonstrating her practical approach to achieving favorable outcomes for clients. She brings to this book her philosophy that a great settlement often surpasses a lengthy court battle, offering readers honest assessments about when to fight and when to explore alternative solutions.

Her legal acumen is evidenced by her work on several notable cases, including *Louis Capital Markets, LP v. Refco Group Ltd., LLC, et al.* (9 Misc.3d 283, 801 N.Y.S.2d 490, N.Y.Co. 2005), which addressed complex issues of corporate espionage, unfair business practices, and employees' fiduciary duties; *Giordano v. Thomson, et al.* (438 F. Supp.2d 35, E.D.N.Y. 2005; 2005 WL 4147932; 2006 WL 1882917); and *Davis v. Commercial Bank of New York* (275 F.Supp.2d 418, S.D.N.Y. 2003), a case involving unwritten ERISA Plans and unjust enrichment.

This guide represents the culmination of Ms. Bolin's extensive experience in both New York and California courts, offering readers an authoritative resource for navigating the complexities of personal injury claims in these two pivotal jurisdictions.

Printed in Dunstable, United Kingdom

91343884R10208